STAGE FAVOURITES OF THE EIGHTEENTH CENTURY

Frontispiece   *By Leslie Blanch*

" To wake the soul by tender strokes of art,
To raise the genius, and to mend the heart."
Pope

STAGE FAVOURITES
OF THE
EIGHTEENTH CENTURY

By
LEWIS S. BENJAMIN
(LEWIS MELVILLE, PSEUD.)

Essay Index Reprint Series

Illustrated

 BOOKS FOR LIBRARIES PRESS
FREEPORT, NEW YORK

First Published 1928
Reprinted 1969

LIBRARY OF CONGRESS CATALOG CARD NUMBER:

68-57303

PRINTED IN THE UNITED STATES OF AMERICA

TO

J. M. BLANCH

CONTENTS

LIST OF ILLUSTRATIONS

ANNE (" NANCE ") OLDFIELD
1683–1730

ANNE ("NANCE") OLDFIELD
1683–1730

ANNE (invariably called "Nance") was thought by Joseph Knight to have been the granddaughter of a vintner, and daughter of a soldier in the Guards. He thought that the father was, perhaps, the James Oldfield of St. Martin's - in - the - Fields, who married Elizabeth Blanchard, of the same parish, on December 4, 1782. According to Edmund Bellchambers, Nance "would have possessed a tolerable fortune, had not her father, a captain in the army, expended it at a very early period." Anyhow, mother and daughter were evidently in very poor circumstances, for as a mere child Nance worked as a seamstress at Westminster, and "lived in." Presently she went to reside with the mother at the Mitre Tavern, St. James's Market. This was kept by a Mrs. Foss, who, one authority says, was Nance's aunt, and another, Dr. Doran, believes to have been Nance's elder sister—in which latter case, unless Elizabeth Blanchard was a widow when she married Oldfield, since Nance was born within a year of that marriage, then Mrs. Foss was illegitimate. Really it seems a shame to take away her good name unnecessarily.

It is said that Nance was from her youth stage-struck, and spent all her spare time reading the plays of Beaumont and Fletcher and others. At the Mitre

Tavern, where, no doubt, she assisted Mrs. Foss in
waiting on the customers, she was overheard by
George Farquhar (who was presently her lover)
reciting passages from *The Scornful Lady*. He was
much impressed by her powers, and praised them
to her mother, who repeated the dramatist's remarks
to his brother-playwright, John Vanburgh, who also
frequented the inn. He, too, thought her clever as
well as pretty, and suggested that she should try
her fortune on the stage. At first she affected coyness ; then she hesitated—she would, she would not.
" I longed to be at it," presently she told William
Rufus Chetwood, sometime prompter at Drury Lane
Theatre, " and only wanted a little decent entreaties."
The entreaties being forthcoming, she yielded to
Vanburgh's wish, and he introduced her to John
Rich, who, anxious to oblige, forthwith gave her an
engagement at the splendid weekly salary of fifteen
shillings a week, which a little later he munificently
increased by five shillings. This was in 1699.

" In the year 1699," Colley Cibber writes : " Mrs.
Oldfield was first taken into the House [*i.e.*, Drury
Lane Theatre], where she remained about a twelvemonth almost mute and unheeded, until Sir John
Vanburgh, who first recommended her, gave her the
part of Alinda in the *Pilgrim* [of Beaumont and
Fletcher] revised. This gentle character happily
became that want of confidence which is inseparable
from young beginners, who, without it, seldom arrive
at any excellence. Notwithstanding, I own I was
then so far deceived in my opinion of her, that I
thought she had little more than her person that
appeared necessary to the forming a good actress ;
for she set out with so extraordinary a diffidence,
that it kept her too despondingly down to a formal,

plain (not to say) flat manner of speaking. Nor could the silver tone of her voice until after some time incline my ear to any hope in her favour. But public approbation is the warm weather of a theatrical plant, which will soon bring it forward to whatever perfection Nature has designed it."

Charles Gildon, in his *Comparison between the Two Stages*, published in 1702, included Nance Oldfield among the " mere rubbish that ought to be swept off the stage with the filth and dust." The actress, however, was soon to prove him wrong.

" Mrs. Oldfield (perhaps for want of fresh parts) seemed to come but slowly forward until the year 1703," Cibber continues. " Our company that summer acted at Bath during the residence of Queen Anne at that place. At that time it happened that Mrs. Verbruggen, by reason of her late sickness (of which she some months after died) was left in London ; and though most of her parts were, of course, to be disposed of, yet so earnest was the female scramble for them, that only one of them fell to the share of Mrs. Oldfield, that of Leonora in *Sir Courtly Nice*, a character of good plain sense, but not over-elegantly written. It was in this part Mrs. Oldfield surprised me into an opinion of her having all the innate powers of a good actress, though they were yet but the bloom of what they promised. Before she had acted this part, I had so cold an expectation from her abilities, that she could scarcely prevail with me to rehearse with her the scene she was chiefly concerned in with Sir Courtly, which I then acted. However, we ran them over with a mutual inadvertency of one another. I seemed careless, as concluding that any assistance I could give her would be to little or no purpose ; and she muttered out her words in a sort of miffty manner at my low opinion of her. But when the play came to be acted, she had a just occasion to triumph over the error of my judgment, by the (almost) amazement that her unexpected performance awaked me to; so forward and sudden a step into nature I had never seen; and what made her performance more valuable was, that I knew it all proceeded from her own understanding, untaught and unassisted by any one more experienced actor."

This was a handsome tribute, and it was sporting of the actor-dramatist to admit his error of judgment.

"Though this part of Leonora in *Sir Courtly Nice* in itself was of so little value, that when she got more into esteem it was one of the several she gave away to inferior actresses," Cibber goes on to say, "yet it was the first (as I have observed) that corrected my judgment of her and confirmed me in a strong belief that she could not fail in very very little time of being what she was afterwards allowed to be, the foremost ornament of our theatre. Upon this unexpected sally, then, of the power and disposition of so unforeseen an actress, it was that I again took up the first two acts of *The Careless Husband*, which I had written the summer before, and had thrown aside in despair of having justice done to the character of Lady Betty Modish by any one woman then among us; Mrs. Verbruggen being now in a very declining state of health, and Mrs. Bracegirdle out of my reach and engaged in another company. But, as I have said, Mrs. Oldfield having thrown out such new proffers of a genius, I was no longer at a loss for support; my doubts were dispelled, and I had a new call to finish it. Accordingly, *The Careless Husband* took its fate upon the stage [at Drury Lane] the winter following, 1704."

ANNE OLDFIELD
Engraving by Simon, after Richardson

Cibber was more than just, he was magnanimous :
" Whatever favourable reception this comedy has
met with from the public, it would be unjust in me
not to place a large share of it to the account of Mrs.
Oldfield ; not only from the uncommon excellence of
her action, but even from her personal manner of
conversing.   There are many sentiments in the
character of Lady Betty Modish that I may almost
say were originally her own, or only dressed with
a little more care when they negligently fell from her
high humour.   Had her birth placed her in a higher
rank of life she had certainly appeared in reality what
in this play she only excellently acted, an agreeable
gay woman of quality a little too conscious of her
natural attractions.

" I have often seen her in private societies, where
women of the best rank might have borrowed some
part of her behaviour without the least diminution of
their sense or dignity.   And this very morning, where
I am now writing at Bath, November 11, 1738, the
same words were said of her by a Lady of Condition,
whose better judgment of her personal merit in that
light has emboldened me to repeat them.   After her
success in this character of higher life, all that Nature
has given her of the actress seemed to have risen to
its full perfection, but the variety of characters ;
which, as fast as they fall to her, she equally excelled
in.   Authors had much more from her performances
than they had reason to hope for from what they had
written for her ; and none had less than another,
but as their genius in the parts they allotted her was
more or less elevated.

" In the wearing of her person she was particularly
fortunate, her figure was always improving to her
thirty-sixth year ; but her excellence in acting was

B

never at a stand ; and the last new character she shone
in [Lady Townly] was a proof that she was still able
to do more, if more could have been done for her. She
had one mark of good sense, rarely known in any
actor of either sex, but herself. I have observed
several, with promising dispositions, very desirous of
instruction at their first setting out ; but no sooner
had they found their least account in it, than they
were as desirous of being left to their own capacity,
which they then thought would be disgraced by their
seeming to want any further assistance. But this
was not Mrs. Oldfield's way of thinking, for, to the
last year of her life, she never undertook any part
she liked without being importunately desirous of
giving all the helps on it that another could possibly
give her. By knowing so much herself, she found
how much more there was of Nature yet to be known.
Yet it is a hard matter to give her any hint that she
was not able to take or improve.

" With all this merit she was tractable and less
presuming in her station than several that had not
half her pretentions to be troublesome ; but she lost
nothing by her easy conduct ; she had everything she
asked, which she took care should be always reasonable, because she hated so much to be grudged as
denied a civility.

" Upon her extraordinary action in *The Provoked
Husband*, the Manager of Drury Lane Theatre made
her a present of fifty guineas more than her agreement, which was never more than a verbal one ; for
they knew she was above deserting them to engage
upon any other stage, and she was conscious they
would never think it their interest to give her cause
of complaint. In the last two months of her illness,
when she was no longer able to assist them, she de-

clined receiving her salary, though by her agreement
she was entitled to it.   Upon the whole she was, to
the last scene she acted, the delight of the spectators."

It is unnecessary to apologise for the above lengthy
extract from Colley Cibber's reminiscences, for no one
knew her better than he.   They must have met
nearly every day for some thirty years at Drury Lane,
at rehearsal during the day, and in the evening at the
performance—for those were not the days of long
runs, and the company was always at work preparing
for the next production.   Clearly she was the ideal
leading lady, even apart from her unquestioned merits
as an actress both in tragedy and comedy, since it is
obvious that she was hard-working, anxious always
to do herself and the author justice, delighting in
fair dealing with her brother and sister artists, never
demanding too much of the limelight for herself,
patient, and courteous to all.

It is not, perhaps, necessary to give a list of the
parts she played.   At first she was almost generally
condemned by the experts, but her inadequacy at
this time was merely the result of lack of experience.
" The rise of Mrs. Oldfield was gradual but secure,
and soon after the death of Mrs. Verbruggen she succeeded to that line of comic parts so happily held by
that popular actress," Bellchambers has written.
" Her Lady Betty Modish, in 1704, before which she
was little known, or barely suffered, discovered
accomplishments the public were not apprised of, and
rendered her one of the greatest favourites upon
whom their sanction had ever been bestowed."

As regards the alleged rivalry between Mrs. Bracegirdle and Nance Oldfield, it is, perhaps, best to quote
that distinguished authority on theatrical history,

Robert W. Lowe, who writes : " It is not until 1691 that Mrs. Bracegirdle can be said to have regularly entered upon her career as an actress. She was the original representative of some of the most famous heroines in comedy : Araminta, in *The Old Batchelor* ; Belinda, in *The Double Dealer* ; Angelica, in *Love for Love* ; Belinda, in *The Provoked Wife* ; Millamont Flippanta, in *The Confederacy*, and many others. Mrs. Bracegirdle appears to have been a good and excellent woman, as well as a great actress. All the scandal about her seems to have no further foundation than, to quote Genest, ' the extreme difficulty with which an actress at this period of the stage must have preserved her chastity.' Mrs. Bracegirdle was perhaps a woman of a cold constitution ! Her retirement from the stage when not much over thirty, is accounted for by Curll, by a story of a competition between her and Mrs. Oldfield in the part of Mrs. Brittle in *The Amorous Widow*, in which the latter was the more applauded. He says that they played the part on two successive nights. I doubt the story altogether. That Mrs. Bracegirdle retired because Mrs. Oldfield was excelling her in popular estimation is most likely, but I can find no confirmation for Curll's story. ' The Laureat ' attributes her retirement to Mrs. Oldfield's being preferred to some parts before her, by our very *Apologist* [*i.e.*, Colley Cibber] ; but though the reason thus given is probably accurate, the person blamed is as probably guiltless ; for I do not think Cibber could have sufficient authority to distribute parts in 1706–7. Mrs. Bracegirdle died September 1748, but was dead to the stage from 1709."

There is to be said, perhaps, in explanation of Nance Oldfield being preferred for certain parts, that she was twenty years younger than Ann Bracegirdle.

Later—but it may as well be mentioned here—there was trouble between Nance Oldfield and Mrs. Rogers, an actress of distinction. When Nance was cast for the character of Andromache in Philips' tragedy, *The Distressed Mother*, which was performed at Drury Lane on March 17, 1712, the supporters of Mrs. Rogers created a disturbance in the theatre. "The only difficulty in Mrs. Oldfield's career," Joseph Knight says, " occurred when she supplanted Mrs. Rogers, who consequently left the theatre in pique. The public, espousing the cause of Mrs. Rogers, hissed Mrs. Oldfield in certain parts. A competition between the two actresses was arranged by the management, and Mrs. Oldfield chose the part of Lady Lurewell in *The Trip to the Jubilee.* Her rival, well advised, withdrew from the contest."

In 1706 Nance left Drury Lane for the "little theatre " in the Haymarket, where she played mostly comedy parts. She returned two years later to Drury Lane ; but soon after returned to the Haymarket, with Swinny, Wilks, Doggett, and Colley Cibber. It may be presumed that these movements were inspired by financial considerations.

Christopher Rich was angry with the seceders, and the Treasurer of Drury Lane, Zachary Baggs, published a manifesto on his behalf, in which Nance Oldfield is pilloried :

£.　s.　d.

"To Mrs. Oldfield, at £4 a week salary, which for fourteen weeks and one day—she leaving off acting, presently after the benefit, *viz. :* on the 17th of March, 1708, though the benefit was intended for her whole nine months acting, and she refused to assist others in their benefits, her salary for these fourteen weeks and one day came to, and she was paid　　56　13　4

" In January she required, and was paid, ten

	£.	s.	d.
guineas, to wear on the stage in some plays			
during the whole season a mantua petticoat			
that was given for the stage, and though she			
left off three months before she should, yet			
she hath not returned any part of the ten			
guineas	10	15	0
" And she had for wearing in some plays a suit			
of boy's clothes on the stage, paid	2	10	9
" By a benefit play, paid	62	7	8."

In 1709 an arrangement was arrived at between
the Managers of Drury Lane Theatre and the members
of the company regularly playing there, on the vexed
question of salaries. As Thomas Doggett, who with
Owen MacSwinny was a joint-director, insisted that
affairs would never be upon a secure foundation if
there was more than one sex admitted to the management, Nance Oldfield was offered a fixed sum per
annum instead of a share. It was feared that she
might feel herself slighted by this proposal, but,
Colley Cibber noted, " she received it rather as a
favour than a disobligation. Her demands, therefore, were two hundred pounds a year certain, and
a benefit clear of all charges, which were readily
signed to. Her easiness on this occasion, some years
after, when our establishment was in prosperity, made
us with less reluctancy advance her two hundred
pounds to three guineas per annum, which with her
usual benefit, upon an average, for several years
at least doubled that sum."

Nance Oldfield in 1711 returned to Drury Lane,
where she stayed for the remainder of her theatrical
career. Her acting, her face and her figure, and her
charm, and, perhaps to some extent, her notoriety as
a woman, made her an immense attraction. " She
was tall, genteel, and well-shaped," Bellchambers

has described her; " her pleasing and expressive
features were enlivened by large speaking eyes, which,
in some particular comic situations, were kept half
shut, especially when she intended to realise some
brilliant idea ; in sprightliness of air, and elegance
of manner, she excelled all actresses ; and was greatly
superior in the strength, compass, and harmony of
her voice." Chetwood has been quite as compli-
mentary : " She was of a superior height, but with
a lovely proportion ; and the dignity of her soul, equal
to her force and character, made up of benevolent
charity, affable, and good-natured to all who deserved
it." Thomas Campbell, the biographer of Mrs.
Siddons, declares that she was " the most beautiful
woman who ever trod the British boards."

Steele was enthusiastic about her : " Flavia," as he
styled her, in *The Spectator*, " is ever well-dressed, and
always the genteelest woman you meet, but the make
of her mind very much contributes to the ornament of
of her body. She has the greatest simplicity of manner
of any of her sex. This makes everything look native
about her, her clothes are so exactly fitted, that they
appear, as it were, part of her person. Everyone
that sees her knows her to be of quality ; but this
distinction is owing to her manner, and not to her
habit. Her beauty is full of attraction, but not of
allurement. There is such a composure in her looks,
and propriety in her dress, that you would think it
impossible she should change the garb you one day
see her in, for anything so becoming, until you next
day see her in another. There is no mystery in this,
but that however she is apparelled, she is herself the
same : for there is so immediate a relation between
our thoughts and gestures, that a woman must think
well to look well." Swift, too, mentions her in his

Journal to Stella, on April 6, 1713, but not so pleasantly:
" I was this morning at the rehearsal of Mr. Addison's
play, called *Cato,* which is to be acted on Friday.
There were not above half a score of us to see it.
We stood on the stage, and it was foolish enough to
see the actors prompted every minute, and the poet
directing them, and the drab [Nance Oldfield] that
acts Cato's daughter, out in the midst of a passionate
part, and then calling out, ' What's next ? ' "

Years later, in 1728, Henry Fielding praised her in
his Preface to *Love in Several Masques* : " After having
returned thanks to the spectators, I cannot rest till
I have been in some measure grateful to the performers.
As for Mr. Wilks and Mr. Cibber, I cannot sufficiently
acknowledge their civil and kind behaviour, previous
to its representation. . . . Lastly, I can never express
my grateful sense of the good-nature of Mrs. Oldfield,
who, though she had contracted a slight indisposition
by her violent fatigue in the part of Lady Townly,
was prevailed upon to grace that of Lady Matchless,
which placed her in a light so far inferior to that
which she had in the other. Nor do I owe less to her
excellent judgment, shown in some corrections, which
I shall, for my own sake, conceal. But the ravishing
perfections of this lady are so much the admiration
of every eye and every ear, that they will remain
fixed in the memory of many, when these light scenes
shall be forgotten."

Of Nance as a comedian, Horace Walpole wrote :
" Who should act genteel comedy perfectly, but
people of fashion who have sense ? Actors and
actresses can only guess at the tone of high life, and
cannot be inspired with it. Why are there so few
genteel comedies, but because most comedies are
written by men not of that sphere. Etheredge, Con-

ANNE OLDFIELD
Painter unknown

greve, Vanbrugh, and Cibber wrote genteel comedy,
because they lived in the best company; and Mrs.
Oldfield played it so well, because she not only followed, but often set, the fashion. General Burgoyne
has writ the best modern comedy for the same reason ;
and Miss Farren is as excellent as Mrs. Oldfield,
because she has lived with the best style of men in
England. Farquhar's plays talk the language of a
marching regiment in country quarters. Wycherley,
Dryden, Mrs. Centlivre, wrote as if they had only
lived in the Rose Tavern ; but then the Court lived
in Drury Lane, too ; and Lady Dorchester and Nell
Gwyn were equally good company."

When Nance Oldfield played Lady Townly in *The
Provoked Husband*, Colley Cibber expressed himself
in the preface to the first edition : " It is not enough
to say, that here she outdid her usual outdoing."
On this, he commented later, " A most vile jingle,
I grant it ! You may ask me, how could I possibly
commit such a wantonness to paper ? And I owe myself the shame of confessing I have no excuse for it,
but that, like a lover in the fulness of his content, by
endeavouring to be floridly grateful, I talked nonsense." In subsequent editions the expression was
changed to, " She here outdid her usual excellence."
Anyhow, the original expression, as, indeed, Cibber
said, expressed his appreciation of the actress's
performance. The revised preface runs :

" There is no doing right to Mrs. Oldfield, without
putting people in mind of what others, of great merit,
have wanted to come near her—it is not enough to
say, she here outdid her usual excellence. I might,
therefore, justly leave her to the constant admiration
of those spectators who have the pleasure of living
while she is an actress. But as this is not the only

time she has been the life of what I have given the
public, so, perhaps, my saying a little more of so
memorable an actress, may give this play a chance
to be read when the people of this age shall be
ancestors. May it, therefore, give emulation to our
successors of the stage, to know that to the ending
of the year 1727, a contemporary comedian relates,
that Mrs. Oldfield was then in her highest excellence
of action, happy in all the rarely found requisites
that meet in one person to complete them for the
stage. She was in stature just rising to that height
where the graceful can only begin to show itself; of
a lively aspect, and a command in her mien, that like
the principal figure in the finest painting, first seizes,
and longest delights the eye of the spectators. Her
voice was sweet, strong, piercing, and melodious, her
pronunciation voluble, distinct, and musical; and
her emphasis always placed where the spirit of the
scene, in her periods, only demanded it. If she
delighted more in the higher comic than in the tragic
strain, it was because the last is too often written
in a lofty disregard of nature. But in characters of
modern practical life, she found occasion to add the
particular air and manner which distinguished the
different humours she presented; whereas in tragedy,
the manner of speaking varies as little as the blank
verse it is written in. She had one peculiar happiness
from Nature, she looked, and maintained, the agreeable at a time when other fine women only raise admirers by their understanding. The spectator was
always as much informed by her eyes as by her elocution; for the look is the only proof that an actor
rightly conceives what he utters, there being scarce
an instance, where the eyes do their part, that the
elocution is known to be faulty. The qualities she

had acquired, were the genteel and the elegant; the one in her air, and the other in her dress, never had her equal on the stage; and the ornaments she herself provided (particularly in this play) seemed in all respects the paraphernalia of a woman of quality. And of that sort were the characters she chiefly excelled in; but her natural good sense and lively turn of conversation made her way so easy to ladies of the highest rank, that it is a less wonder if she sometimes was, what might have become, the finest woman in real life to have supported."

Nance Oldfield suffered much from ill-health during her later years, but she acted even when tears were streaming down her eyes from pain. The last part she created was Sophonisba in Thomson's *Sophonisba*. She took a benefit on March 19, 1730, choosing *The Fair Penitent*, presumably playing Calista, one of her favourite rôles, and on the following April 28, she made her last appearance—as Lady Brute in *The Provoked Husband*.

It may here be mentioned that according to the *General Biographical Dictionary*: " She always went to the theatre in the same dress she had worn at dinner in her visits to the houses of great people; for she was much caressed on account of her general merit, and her connection with Mr. Churchill. She used to go to the playhouse in a chair, attended by two footmen. She seldom spoke to any of the actors, and was allowed a sum of money to buy her own clothes."

Nance Oldfield was far from immaculate as a woman, but everyone was anxious to be kind to her. " Even her amours seemed to lose that glare which appears round the persons of the failing fair," Chetwood writes; " neither was it ever known that she troubled the repose of any lady's lawful claim ; and was far more constant than millions in the conjugal noose." One of her lovers was Arthur Mainwaring (or Maynwaring), and Oldnixon wrote of them, that "each of them loved with a passion that could hardly have been stronger, had it been both her and his first love "—which no doubt he meant kindly. When exactly the intimacy was contracted is not known, but it probably was in or about 1704. He was pamphleteer and politician, and a man of wide acquaintance with literature and a considerable position in society. He became a Commissioner of Customs, and in 1705 Godolphin appointed him Auditor of Imprests, to which office was attached the handsome salary of £3000 a year. He had no sense of money, and left at his death in 1712 but a small property. He appointed Mrs. Oldfield his executrix; and left his estate equally to his sister, to her, and to the son of the *liaison*, Arthur.

After the death of Mainwaring, his place in Nance's affections was then—or perhaps earlier—taken by General Charles Churchill, a son of Sir Winston Churchill, a brother of John, first Duke of Marlborough. By him, too, she had a son. It is said they were married, and that one day when she was at Court, presumably reading a play, the Queen said to her, " I hear, Mrs. Oldfield, that you and the General are married "—to which the actress replied cryptically, " Ma'am, the General keeps his own secrets " ; or, according to another version, " So it is said, Ma'am, but we have not owned it yet." However, nobody seemed to care whether they were married or not, and she was received in society, and in her turn entertained them at her house. Her son, Colonel Charles Churchill, once saved Sir Robert Walpole from assassination, through the latter riding home from

the House of Commons in the Colonel's chariot instead
of alone in his own.   Colonel Churchill married a
natural daughter of Sir Robert, and their daughter,
Mary, married in 1777 Charles Sloane, first Earl of
Cadogan.   When Churchill and his wife were travelling
in France, a Frenchman, knowing he was connected
with poets or players, asked him if he was Churchill,
the famous poet.   " I am not," said Mrs. Oldfield's
son.   " *Ma foi !* " rejoined the polite Frenchman,
" so much the worse for you."

Nance Oldfield died in London at the age of forty-
seven, on October 23, 1730, at her house, No. 59
(afterwards 60) Grosvenor Street.   According to her
maid, Margaret Saunders, she was interred in " a very
fine Brussels lace head, a holland shift, and double
ruffles of the same lace, a pair of new kid gloves, and
her body wrapped in a winding sheet."   To this
Pope referred in his " Moral Essays " :

> " Odious ! in woollen ! 'twould a saint provoke
> (Were the last words that poor Narcissa spoke) ;
> No, let a charming chintz and Brussels lace
> Wrap my cold limbs, and shade my lifeless face :
> One would not sure, be frightful when one's dead—
> And—Betty—give this cheek a little red."

Pope referred to her also in " Sober Advice from
Horace " :

> " Engaging Oldfield ! who, with grace and ease,
> Could join the arts to ruin and to please."

Nance Oldfield is probably the only actress who
has lain in state in the Jerusalem Chamber, and it is
difficult to imagine how this came to pass.   The chief
mourner at her funeral was her elder illegitimate son,
Arthur Mainwaring ; and the pall-bearers were Lord
de la Warr, Lord Hervey of Ickworth (husband of the

beautiful " Molly " Lepell), George Bubb Dodington (afterwards Lord Melcombe), Charles Hedges, Walter Carey, and Captain Elliot. She was buried beneath the monument of Congreve in Westminster Abbey. An application by General Churchill for permission to erect a monument to her in the Abbey was refused by the Dean.

Richard Savage, to whom she had been very kind, wrote the following lines on her :

> " Oldfield's no more ! and can the Muse forbear
> O'er Oldfield's grave to shed a grateful tear ?
> Shall she, the glory of the British stage,
> Pride of her sex, and wonder of the age ;
> Shall she, who, living, charm'd th' admiring throng,
> Die undistinguish'd, and not claim a song ?
> No ! feeble as it is, I'll boldly raise
> My willing voice to celebrate her praise,
> And with her name immortalize my lays.
> Had but my Muse her art to touch the soul,
> Charm ev'ry sense, and ev'ry pow'r control,
> I'd paint her as she was—the form divine,
> Where ev'ry lovely grace united shine ;
> A mien majestic, as the wife of Jove ;
> An air as winning as the Queen of Love ;
> In ev'ry feature rival charms should rise,
> And Cupid hold his empire in her eyes.
> A soul, with ev'ry elegance refin'd
> By Nature and the converse of mankind ;
> Wit, which could strike assuming folks dead,
> And sense, which temper'd eve'ry thing she said ;
> Judgment, which ev'ry little fault could spy ;
> But candour, which would pass a thousand by.
> Such finish'd breeding, so polite a taste,
> Her fancy always for the fashion pass'd ;
> Whilst every social virtue fir'd her breast,
> To help the needy, succour the distrest.
> A friend to all in misery she stood,
> And her chief pride was plac'd in doing good.
> But now, my Muse, the arduous task engage,
> And shew the charming figure on the stage ;

Describe her look, her action, voice, and mien,
The gay coquette, soft-maid, or haughty Queen.
So bright she shone, in ev'ry different part,
She gain'd despotic empire o'er the heart ;
Knew how each various motion to control,
Soothe ev'ry passion, and subdue the soul.
As she, o'er gay or sorrowful appears,
She claims our mirth, or triumphs in our tears.
When Cleopatra's form she chose to wear,
We saw the monarch's mien, the beauty's air ;
Charmed with the sight, her cause we all approve,
And, like her lover, give up all for love :
Anthony's fate, instead of Cæsar's, choose,
And wish for her we had a world to lose.
But now the gay, delightful scene is o'er,
And that sweet form must glad our world no more ;
Relentless death has stop'd the tuneful tongue,
And clos'd those eyes, for all, but death, too strong,
Blast'd that face where ev'ry beauty bloom'd,
And to Eternal Rest the graceful Mover doom'd."

LAVINIA FENTON (*née* **BESWICK)**
afterwards **DUCHESS OF BOLTON**
1708–1760

LAVINIA FENTON (*née* BESWICK) *afterwards* DUCHESS OF BOLTON

1708-1760

THE original of Polly Peachum in *The Beggar's Opera*, by Mr. Gay! That is fame indeed, enduring fame in the annals of the theatre.

Lavinia was born in 1708. According to Mr. Gordon Goodwin, her reputed father was a lieutenant in the navy named Beswick, who having to return to duty before the child was born, left the injunction that if it should be a boy, it should be named Porteus; if a girl, it was his pleasure that she should be called Lavinia—why, he alone knew! However, his injunction was respected—there is no record of his further interesting himself in his illegitimate offspring. Of the mother about as much, and not more, is known of her. She married a man called Fenton in the Old Bailey, and started a coffee-house not far from Charing Cross. She bestowed the surname of her husband upon her daughter, perhaps it made for respectability.

" Mrs. Fenton, being a woman of a popular spirit, soon after her marriage set up a coffee-house in Charing Cross, where Polly being a child of a vivacious, lively spirit, and of promising beauty, was a plaything for the fops. She never failed to afford them an agreeable diversion, and though at this time she was but seven or eight years of age, she had some singular talents of wit, which showed her of an aspiring genius, and one that would in time strive with emulation to exceed the bounds of her narrow fortune. It was about this time that a comedian belonging to the Old House [Drury Lane] took great delight in hearing her sing little catches as she had heard from the humming beaux, or the more lofty strains of her Mamma, by whose intercession this gentleman took a great deal of pains with Polly and taught her some airs which have since been to her advantage, and in which she daily improved, till her mother sent her to a boarding school, where she stayed till she was fourteen, and then came home again to live with her mother, who was removed once more into the Old Bailey."

The above passage is taken from a catchpenny biography, published in 1728, entitled *The Life of Lavinia Beswick*, alias *Fenton*, alias *Polly Peachum*. It is most probably entirely unreliable, and the only excuse for making some quotations from it is that there is no other early biographical information about the lady. This is the less surprising because she went on the stage when she was eighteen and retired two years later. " The Life " speaks openly of her youthful amours.

" A gallant spark of the Inner Temple, seeing her one night at a ball, fell deeply in love with her, and took occasion to let her know it, both by letter and personal application ; and though she was scarce thirteen, she felt such emotions for young *Noverint Universi* that she suffered the servant to take bribes to let him into the garden, and would frequently bless him with an hour's conversation. And here it is said (by those who are acquainted with her most private actions from her infancy to this time) that she fell as deeply in love with the Templer, as he could possibly be with her ; yet she had ever that discretion

to make a distinction between the secret impulses of
her heart, and the expressions of the tongue, daily
feeling by experience, that when a woman lets the
sentiments of her soul out at her lips, her love is
counted fondness, and the man who was ready to die
at her feet will be ready to stigmatise her for a good-
natured fool. Hypocrisy being now made a necessary
ingredient in affairs of love, and downright dealing
the only impediment that can make a promising view
prove abortive ; she therefore kept him at a convenient
distance, and seemed to give way to his courtship
only, as a grateful complaisance to a man that merited
something which she was incapable of granting.
And with this pretended indolent Templer she made
use of that infallible net for catching men in love,
a killing coyness ! Poor Polly ! The spark happening
in company where her name was mentioned, took
occasion to inquire into her private affairs, and finding
her birth and fortune were such as would but bring
a disgrace to his family, he left her.

 " This disappointment made such an impression
in her mind that the company at the boarding-school
became burdensome, and the pleasant garden where
she used to delight herself with the young lawyer
intolerable, and as an expedient to wear off the dilemma
she lay under, she left the school and came home to her
mother, who found her daughter's temper altered from
the gay to the melancholy. She took her to the Park,
the play, and to all entertainments that might conduce
to recover her former vivacity.

 " About that time her mother had an intrigue upon
her hands which began at the playhouse and ended
in the bedchamber. . . . But whilst the mother was
thus bargaining for her ware, Polly was no less active
in providing for herself. A Portuguese nobleman,

being her only favourite, she consented, unknown to her mother, to give him the prize, which he generously rewarded ; and, accordingly, on a Friday, in the year 1725, he sent his own coach into the Old Bailey by appointment ; and after the coach had waited three hours, she went into it, and was carried to the place of assignation, where the nobleman kept her till the Monday following, and then sent her home again in the same coach. But this person being unhappy in his private affairs, after some time spent in raptures at his own house, he brought her to her mother, and promised he would make a provision for her, suitable to the merits of so fine a creature. And to do him justice, his generosity was above his patrimony, insomuch that his stock was exhausted, before his appetite palled; and falling into the hands of some severe creditors, he was arrested and carried to the Fleet.

" Whilst the Portuguese nobleman lay confined in the Fleet, a mercer's apprentice who now keeps a shop of that business near the Royal Exchange, then living upon Ludgate Hill fell deeply in love with Polly. Seeing her one night at the playhouse, the poor smitten spark was so captivated at first sight of her that he could scarce forbear making love to her before the face of the whole audience ; his colour went and came, he sighed, trembled, and in short felt all those emotions which men in love are subject to. After the play was over, he watched her into a coach, and lest he should miss her in a throng of whirligigs, he very orderly got up behind, and was set down at her door in the Old Bailey ; but his love was so strong, as deprived him of any other strength, insomuch that when Polly stepped out of the coach into the house, his soul was near stepping out of his

body, he was so far overcome by his amorous passion.
All night he waited about the door, sometimes sighing,
and sometimes raving, fearing she was a married
woman; or doubtless, if she were not, such a fine
creature as she was, would repulse him being but a
lad, and not out of his apprenticeship. But when the
morning came, he was eased from part of his pain;
for upon enquiry after her, he found that she was a
single woman; and at the same time he heard who
she was, that she was a person of a noble mind, though
but of narrow fortune, which did not put the least
damp to him, he having a pretty handsome estate,
when he came of age, and was willing to lay both that
and himself at her feet, and the next day he picked
up a little courage (yet with a heart almost broken for
fear of a denial) and went to inform her of his passion.

" Polly, who had ever a great wit, as well as good
manners, received him like a gentleman, and entertained him very courteously; but at the same time she
assured him, though he came with seeming honourable
pretensions, for which she could but use him with
civility, yet there were some private reasons which
would keep her from a married state, and make his
pretensions to her of none effect."

The following is a letter printed in " The Life,"
purporting to have been written to Lavinia by a
young ensign :

" MADAM,

" You may be a person of honour, for aught
I know to the contrary, and I hope you will be so
honourable as not to let a man of honour die dis-
honourably at your feet. For, by Heavens! though
I thought nothing so bright as my sword, yet I find
your eyes are much brighter. My dear, dear Guardian

Angel, could you conceive the anxiety I suffer on your account, you would surely pity me : for there is never an officer of our Regiment but takes notice of my being changed (since I saw you upon the stage) from the most lively, brisk, fashionable, mannerly, genteel Beau in the whole army, to the most dull, insipid, slovenly, out-of-the-way-tempered dunce in Christendom. D—n me, Madam, if I am not so over-charged with love that my heart, which is the bullet in the barrel of my body, will certainly burst and blow me into atoms if I have not your help to discharge the burden. And then Blood ! Madam, I am guilty of so many blunders and mistakes in the execution of my office that I am become quite a laughing-stock to the whole army. Yesterday I put my sword on the wrong side, and this morning came into the Park with one of my stockings the wrong side outward, and instead of applying myself to the Colonel, in the usual terms of Most Noble Sir, I looked pale, and with an affected d—d cringe, called him, Madam. Thus, Madam, you see how far I am gone already. Then to keep me from Bedlam, take me to your arms, then I will lay down my arms, and be your slave and vassal."

Actually, then, nothing is really known about Lavinia until 1726, when she made her first appear-ance on the stage as Monomia in Otway's *The Orphan* at the new theatre in the Haymarket. How she came to decide upon, or drift into, a theatrical career none can say. It may be that one of her lovers —for lovers, in her circumstances, may be presumed— was more or less directly connected with the theatre. She did not long remain at the Haymarket—indeed, she was only there a few weeks—but joined a company of comedians who played twice a week at the theatre

LAVINIA FENTON
By Tenney

in Lincoln's Inn Fields. Presently, James Rich, the manager of that theatre, gave her an engagement for the winter season of 1727–28 at a salary of fifteen shillings a week : even when she was drawing all the town as Polly Peachum in *The Beggar's Opera* which "made Gay rich and Rich gay," she only drew thirty shillings a week. That she had made good on the stage is clearly demonstrated by the fact that with, so far as is known, only eighteen months or so of experience she should have been cast for that character.

The Beggar's Opera was produced on January 29, 1728. It is believed that the first suggestion of it had come from Swift, in a letter to Pope, written so far back as 1716. " Dr. Swift has been observing once to Mr. Gay, what an odd, pretty thing a Newgate Pastoral might make," Pope once remarked. " Gay was inclined to try at such a thing for some time, but afterwards thought it better to write a comedy on the same plan. This was what gave rise to *The Beggar's Opera*. He began on it, and when first he mentioned it to Swift, the Doctor did not much like the project. As he carried it on, he showed what he wrote to both of us ; and we now and then gave a correction, or a word or two of advice ; but it was wholly of his own writing. When it was done, neither of us thought it would succeed. We showed it to Congreve, who, after reading it, said : ' It would either take greatly, or be damned confoundedly.' " Gay has given his own account of the inception of his opera : " This piece, I own, was originally written for the celebrating the marriage of James Chanter and Moll Lay, two most excellent ballad singers : I have introduced the similes that are in all your celebrated operas : the Swallow, the Moth, the Bee, the Ship, the

Flower, etc. Besides, I have a prison scene, which the ladies always reckon charmingly pathetic. As to the parts, I have observed such a nice impartiality to our two ladies, that it is impossible for either of them to take offence. I hope I may be forgiven that I have not made my opera throughout unnatural, like those in vogue ; for I have no recitative ; excepting this, as I have consented to have neither prologue or epilogue, it must be allowed an opera in all its forms. The piece indeed has been heretofore frequently represented by ourselves in our room at St. Giles's, so that I cannot too often acknowledge your charity in bringing it now on the stage."

The original cast was as follows :

Peachum	Mr. Hippisley
Lockit	Mr. Hall
Macheath	Mr. Walker
Fitch	Mr. Clark
Jemmy Twitcher	Mr. H. Bullock
Mrs. Peachum	Mrs. Martin
Polly Peachum	Miss Fenton
Lucy Lockit	Mrs. Egleton
Diana Trapes	Mrs. Martin

At the first performance the fate of the opera hung for some time in the balance. Not only Swift, Pope, and Congreve were doubtful as to its success, but Colley Cibber had declined it for Drury Lane ; and even when it was accepted by John Rich for the theatre in Lincoln's Inn Fields, James Quin had such a poor opinion of it that he refused the part of Macheath. It is recorded that Quin said that there was a disposition to damn it, and that it was saved by the song, " O ponder well ! be not severe ! " the audience being much affected by the innocent looks of Polly Peachum when she came to those lines which at once exhibit such a painful and ridiculous image :

> " O ponder well ! be not severe !
> For on the Rope that hangs my Dear,
> Depends poor Polly's Life."

Most of Gay's friends were present. "We," wrote Pope, "were all at the first night of it, in great uncertainty of the event, till we were very much encouraged by hearing the Duke of Argyll, who sat in the next box to us, say : ' It will do—it must do—I see it in the eyes of them.' This was a good while before the first act was over, and gave us ease soon ; for the Duke (besides his own good taste) has a more particular knack than anyone now living, in discovering the taste of the public. He was quite right in this, as usual. The good nature of the audience appeared stronger and stronger every act, and ended in a clamour of applause."

The success of the opera was due to several causes. Some liked it for its barely veiled allusions to politicians. Robin of Bagshot, *alias* Gorgon, *alias* Bluff Bob, *alias* Carbuncle, *alias* Bob Booty, was very obviously intended for Sir Robert Walpole, and the "Dear charmers" for his wife and "Molly Skerrett," his mistress. It may well be believed that the song,

> " How happy could I be with either
> Were t'other dear charmer away ! "

brought down the house ; and the highwayman must have evoked a hearty laugh with

> " And the statesman, because he's so great,
> Thinks his trade as honest as mine."

The success of the evening was unquestionably Lavinia Fenton. "The person who acted Polly

Peachum," said the anonymous editor of *Plays written by Mr. John Gay,* in 1760, "till then obscure, became all at once the favourite of the town ; her pictures were engraved, and sold in great numbers ; her life written ; books of letters and verses to her published ; and pamphlets made even of her sayings and jests."

"There is a mezzotinto print published to-day of Polly, the heroine of *The Beggar's Opera,*" Gay wrote in high glee to Swift on March 29, 1728, " who was before unknown, and is now in so high vogue that I am in doubt whether her fame does not surpass that of the opera itself."

There appeared the biography to which reference has been made : the title is almost a volume in itself :

" The Life of Lavinia Beswick, *alias* Fenton, *alias* Polly Peachum : containing, Her Birth and Education. Her Intrigues at a Boarding School. Her first acquaintance with a certain *Portugueze* Nobleman. The Time when, and the Person to whom she bestow'd her first Favours. A particular Account of her Conversation with a Mercer, now living near the *Royal Exchange.* Of the *Portugueze* Nobleman being confin'd in the *Fleet,* and the honourable Method she took to give him his Liberty. A copy of Verses which she composed on a *Fop,* which conduced to her Acquaintance with Mr. *Huddy,* for whose Benefit, at the New Theatre in the *Hay-Market,* she first appear'd on the Stage. A particular Account of a Benefit she shar'd with one Mr. Gilbert, a few Weeks after Mr. *Huddy's,* at the same Theatre. Her first Admittance into the Theatre-Royal in *Lincoln's-Inn-Fields :* Her weekly Salary, both now and then ; and the Time when, and the cause why, it was raised. Of her Wit gaining her more Lovers than her Beauty. The Horse-Courser dismounted, yet saves his Distance. A Poet strutting under the protection of the Nine Muses. Another poet, who would attack *Ulysses* and *Penelope* in a barbarous Manner, is severely handled by *Polly* in a Satirical Stanza. Her judgment in Poetry and History Painting. And the remarkable reason why so many great men have been her humble servants. The whole interspers'd with convincing Proofs of her *Ingenuity*, *Wit*, and *Smart* Repartees, and concluding with some remarkable Instances of her *Humanity* to the *Distressed*. London : Printed for A. Moore, near St. Paul's ; and sold by the Booksellers and Pamphlet-Shops in *London* and *Westminster*. 1728. (*Price*, One Shilling.) ”

Besides the above, was published in the same year— though the second edition is unaccountably dated 1727 on the title-page—“ Letters in Prose and Verse to the celebrated Polly Peachum from the Most Eminent of the Admirers and Rivals ” ; and numerous lampoons. “ A new Ballad inscrib'd to Polly Peachum” is too lewd for reproduction ; but the reply may be printed :

“ AN ANSWER TO POLLY PEACHUM'S BALLAD.

“ The following lines being sent to the author as an answer to the foregoing ballad, he to shew what he published was not done out of malice to Polly Peachum, has annexed them to this edition, having so much value for the female sex as to give them fair play to a fair woman.

“ Pray, Sir, who are you
That thus dares to shew
Polly's pranks to open view
And as loudly expose her.
Cruel bard,
This is hard
No regard
To Poll, or those who know her ;
For you do lampoon 'em all,
For you do lampoon 'em all,
As well as pretty Poll.

" Are you pimp or spy
That does thus decry
Poll's gallants, and where they lie,
L——s and G——'d cullies :
Can't your muse
Something choose
From the stews
Of common whores and bullies ;
But maliciously you fall,
But maliciously you fall,
On pretty, pretty Poll.

" Poll performs her parts
With such grace and art,
That every night she conquers hearts,
Both in pit and boxes.
Then refrain,
Be'nt so plain,
Do not stain
Poll with common doxies
For she does charm us all,
For she does charm us all,
O, pretty, pretty Poll.

" Since Poll has gain'd applause,
All vindicate her cause,
And prodigious crowds she draws,
All conspire to clap her ;
The house rings
When she sings.
Must such thanks
Vanish in a vapour ?
No, she outshines them all,
No, she outshines them all,
O, pretty pretty Poll."

The following was written by Henry Carey, to be sung to the air of his own " Sally in Our Alley " :

" POLLY PEACHUM.

" Of all the toasts that Britain boasts,
The gin, the gent, the jolly,
The brown, the fair, the debonnaire,
There's none cry'd up like Polly.

She's fir'd the town, has quite cut down
   The Opera of Rolti :
Go where you will, the subject still,
   Is pretty, pretty Polly.

" There's Madam Faustina Catso !
   And the Madame Catsoni
Likewise Signior Senesino,
   Are *tutti abbandonni*,
Ha, ha, ha, ha !   *Do re mi fa*,
   Are now but Farce and Folly
We're ravished all with Toll, loll, loll,
   And pretty, pretty Polly.

" The sons of Bayes in lyric lays,
   Sounds forth her fame in print O !
And, as we pass, in frame and glass,
   We see her *Mezzo-tint-O !*
In Ivy Lane the City strain
   Is now no more on Dolly,
And all the brights at *Man's* and *White's*
   Of nothing talk but Polly.

" Ah, Johnny Gay ! thy lucky play
   Has made the critics gain, a ;
They cry, 'tis flat, 'tis this, 'tis that
   But let them laugh that win, a.
I swear Parbleu, 'tis naif and new,
   Ill nature is but Folly ;
Has lent a stitch to rent of Rich,
   And set up Madam Polly.

" Ah, tuneful Fair ! Beware ! Beware !
   Nor toy with Star and Garter ;
Fine clothes may hide a foul inside
   And you may catch a Tartar :
If powder'd fop blow up your shop,
   'Twill make you melancholy ;
Then left to rot, you'll die forgot,
   Alas ! Alas ! poor Polly."

June 14, 1728, was set aside for Lavinia Fenton's
benefit, and she elected to play Cherry in *The Beaux's*

Stratagem. There was trouble about the benefit, however, for Lavinia Fenton, no doubt anxious to have as profitable a house as possible, sold box and pit seats indiscriminately at the same price, with the result that many who had bought seats in the boxes and received vouchers for the stalls returned their tickets—an almost inconceivable error of judgment. However, Rich, good-naturedly, took the receipts of that night for himself; and gave her a second benefit on the following May 4, when *The Beggar's Opera* was played for the forty-seventh time.

Lavinia Fenton played in all the sixty-two performances of the opera, the last taking place on June 19, 1728, after which she left the stage for ever—a glorious career, in spite of its brevity.

" The Duke of Bolton, I hear," Gay wrote to Swift, " has run away with Polly Peachum, having settled £400 a year on her during pleasure, and upon disagreement £200 a year." As regards the settlement, Gay was probably only repeating the gossip of the day ; but the fact could not be disputed. Charles Paulet, eldest son of Charles, second Duke of Bolton, was born in 1685, and, therefore, was twenty-three years older than his mistress. He sat in the House of Commons from 1705 until 1717, when he was summoned by writ to the House of Lords, with the title of Lord Basing. He was at this time a Lord of the Bedchamber to the Prince of Wales, and Colonel of the royal regiment of Horse-Guards. His father in 1713 insisted—under threat of partial disinheritance, or stoppage of allowance, presumably—upon his marrying Lady Anne Vaughan, only daughter and heiress of John, Earl of Carbery. So soon as Charles came into the title—in 1722—he, no longer suffering under the threat of disinheritance, separated from his wife,

LAVINIA FENTON AS POLLY PEACHUM IN
"THE BEGGAR'S OPERA"
By Hogarth

who had not given him an heir. When he was first attracted by Lavinia Fenton cannot be definitely stated ; but it would appear that this was years later, when she was playing in *The Beggar's Opera*. The pair lived openly together. " An honest, tender mind," wrote Lady Mary Wortley Montagu, " is betrayed to ruin by the charms that make the fortune of a designing head, which, when joined with a beautiful face, can never fail of advancement, except barred by a wise mother, who locks up her daughters from view, until no one cares to look on them." She instanced the case of " my poor friend, the Duchess of Bolton, who was educated in solitude, with some choice books, by a saint-like governess ; crammed with virtue and good qualities, she thought it impossible not to find gratitude, though she failed to give passion ; and upon this plan threw away her estate, was despised by her husband, and laughed at by the public." Lady Mary compared the case of the Duchess with that of " Polly, bred in an ale-house, but produced on the stage, who has obtained wealth and title, and found the way to be esteemed. So useful is early experience."

Anyhow the liaison was satisfactory to both parties. Until the Duke's death, they were rarely apart for any length of time. When the death of the Duchess was expected, they went abroad, and took with them the Rev. Dr. Joseph Warton, the friend of Johnson and his circle, who accompanied them as chaplain to his Grace, so as to be on the spot to marry the lovers at the earliest possible moment. The clergyman said of the lady : " She was very accomplished ; was a most agreeable companion ; had much wit, and strong sense, and a just taste in polite literature." Can it be that Lavinia had praised his " Odes " ?

D

Anyhow, he continued, " Her person was agreeable and well-made, though she could not be called a beauty. I have had the pleasure of being at table with her, when her conversation was much admired by the first characters of the age, particularly the old Lord Bathurst and Lord Granville." After the death of the Duchess, the Duke married his mistress at Aix in Provence, on September 20, 1751, after a connection with her of thirty-three years. He had by her three sons while they were living together ; but no children after their marriage. He was, therefore, succeeded in the dukedom by his brother.

Having already made ample provision for his natural children by Lavinia Fenton, he left all the property at his disposal to his " dear and well-beloved wife." The Duchess survived until 1760, being then in her fifty-eighth year.

CATHERINE ("KITTY") CLIVE, *née* RAFTOR

1711–1785

CATHERINE ("KITTY") CLIVE
née RAFTOR
1711-1785

KITTY CLIVE is still a name to conjure with, though it is nearly a hundred and fifty years since her death. Wayward, quarrelsome, yet kind-hearted, her charms subdued all with whom she came in contact during the seventy-four years of her life—excepting only her husband. Even Charles Churchill wrote kindly of her, and Horace Walpole adored her.

The sole authority for the parentage and early years of Catherine Raftor is William Chetwood: " This celebrated natural actress was the daughter of Mr. William Raftor, a gentleman born in the city of Kilkenny, Ireland. The father of her father was possessed of a considerable paternal estate in the county where he was born; but the parents of our actress being unhappily attached to the unfortunate King James the Second, the late Revolution gave it, among many others, to the Crown. Mr. James Raftor, her brother, went over to Ireland some years ago, in order to solicit for his grandfather's fortune, but did not meet with success. Mr. William Raftor, the father, was tied to the law; however, when King James was in Ireland, he entered into his service, and after the decisive Battle of the Boyne in the year 1690, he followed his master's fortune, and by his merit

obtained a captain's commission in the service of Louis
the Fourteenth ; but gaining a pardon, with many
other gentlemen in his condition, he came to England,
where he married Miss Daniel, daughter of an eminent
citizen on Fish Street Hill, with whom he had a handsome fortune. By her he had a numerous issue.
Miss Catherine was born in 1711. She had an early
genius for the stage, for she told me, when she was
about twelve years old, Miss Johnston (afterwards
Mrs. Theo. Cibber, another rising genius, if death had
not overtaken her in the prime of youth), and she used
to tag after the celebrated Mr. Wilks (her own words)
wherever they saw him in the streets, and gape at
him as a wonder. Miss Raftor had a facetious turn
of humour and infinite spirit, with a voice and manner
in singing songs of pleasantry peculiar to herself."

This may be supplemented by Lee Lewes's account
of her first years in London : " She was originally
servant to Miss Eleanor Knowles, afterwards Mrs.
Young, mother to the present Sir George Young and
Mr. Thomas Young, who in 1774 came out at Covent
Garden Theatre in Macheath which he performed some
nights with much celebrity. When Mrs. Clive lived
with Mrs. Knowles, who then lodged at Mrs. Snell's,
a fan-painter in Church Row, Houndsditch, Mr.
Watson, many years box-keeper at Drury Lane and
Richmond, kept the Bell Tavern opposite to Mrs.
Snell's. At this house was held the Beefsteak Club,
instituted by Mr. Beard, Mr. Dunstall, Mr. Woodward,
etc. Kitty Raftor, being one day *washing the steps
of the house*, and singing, the windows of the club room
being open, they were instantly crowded by the company, who were all enchanted with her natural grace
and simplicity. This circumstance alone led her
to the stage, under the auspices of Mr. Beard and

Mr. Dunstall. . . . I have given the above anecdote as I received it from Mr. Thomas Young."

Why Kitty came to London is not known, for her relations remained in Ireland. Sir Theodore Martin has suggested that perhaps it was because the Raftor family was probably too large for its means, " for," he adds, " all we know of Kitty Clive points to the conclusion that her education was of the scantiest. Her spelling to the last was bad even for the eighteenth century. What she wrote, however, was marked by strong common sense, and she made her way to eminence by sheer force of genius, in spite of a refinement which was incompatible with good early culture." Yet she must have made good some of the defects of her lack of education in her youth, for, ill-spelt as they were, she could, and did write quite good letters. And more, she wrote four dramatic sketches : *The Rehearsal, or, Bays in Petticoats, Every Woman in her Humour*, and *Sketch of a Fine Lady's return from a Rout.*"

There is no doubt that from an early age Kitty hankered after the theatre. It has been said that she was taught music by Henry Carey, the composer of the immortal " Sally in our Alley." Mrs. Theophilus Cibber thought she had the necessary qualifications for the stage, and she and Chetwood recommended her to Colley Cibber, the manager of Drury Lane Theatre, " whose infallible judgment," says Chetwood, " soon found out her excellencies. The moment he heard her sing, he put her down in his list of performers at twenty shillings a week." This was five shillings a week more than the first salary of Lavinia Fenton.

Kitty Raftor joined the company at Drury Lane when she was seventeen, in 1728—the year of the

production of *The Beggar's Opera*. She first appeared
in Nat Lee's *Mithridates, King of Pontius*, as Ismenes,
page to Ziphares, and she sang a song by Sir Car
Scroop written for the piece. She scored an immediate
success. In October of that year she was cast for
Bianca in *Othello* ; and in November took part in the
same evening in a comedy, *Æsop*, in which the
title-rôle was undertaken by Cibber, and in " a new
dramatic entertainment of dancing in serious and
grotesque characters," called *Perseus and Andro-
meda, with the Rape of Columbine, or, The Flying
Lovers*. In January, 1729, she played Dorinda in
The Tempest ; and was generally kept busy with
a variety of parts.

Kitty Raftor's next great success was as Phillida
in Colley Cibber's ballad opera, *Love in a Riddle*.
" After the vast success of that new species of dramatic
poetry, *The Beggar's Opera*, the year following, I was
so stupid, as to attempt something of the same kind
upon quite a different foundation, that of recommend-
ing virtue and innocence, which I ignorantly thought
might not have a less pretence to favour, than setting
greatness and authority in a contemptible light,"
Colley Cibber wrote in his *Apology*. " But behold
how fondly I was mistaken ! *Love in Riddle* (for so
my new-fangled performance was called) was vilely
damn'd and hooted at as so vain a presumption in the
idle cause of virtue could deserve. Soon after this
prohibition, my performance was to come upon the
stage, at a time, when many people were out of humour
at the late disappointment, and seemed to lay hold
of any pretence of making a reprisal. Great umbrage
was taken that I was permitted to have the whole town
to myself, by this absolute forbidance of what they
had more mind to have been entertained with ; and

CATHERINE CLIVE
By Hogarth

some few days before my bawble was acted, I was
informed that a strong party would be made against it :
this report I slighted, as not conceiving why it should
be true, and when I was afterwards told, what was
the pretended provocation of this party, I slighted it.
The report it seems that had run against me was this :
That, to make way for the success of my own play,
I had privately found means, or made interest, that
the second part of *The Beggar's Opera* might be suppressed. I had not considered, poor devil ! that, from
the security of a full pit, dunces might be critics,
cowards valiant, and apprentices gentlemen ! Whether
any such were concerned in the murder of my play,
I am not certain, for I never endeavoured to discover
any one of the assassins ; I cannot afford them a milder
name, from their unmanly manner of destroying it.
'Tis true, it faintly held up its wounded head, a
second day, and would have spoke for mercy, but
was not suffered. Not even the presence of a royal
heir-apparent could protect it. But then I was reduced
to be serious with them ; their clamour then became
an insolence, which I thought it my duty, by the sacrifice of any interest of my own, to put an end to. I
therefore quitted the actor for the author, and stepping
forward to the pit, told them that since I found they
were not inclined that this play should go forward,
I gave them my word, that after this night, it should
never be acted again : but that in the meantime,
I hoped they would consider in whose presence they
were, and for that reason at least, would suspend
what further marks of their displeasure they might
imagine I had deserved. At this there was a dead
silence ; and after some little pause, a few civilised
hands signified their approbation. When the play
went on, I observed about a dozen persons of no extra-

ordinary appearance sullenly walked out of the pit,
after which, every scene of it, while uninterrupted,
met with more applause than my best hopes had expected. But it came too late : Peace to its manes ! "

" I remember the first night of *Love in a Riddle*
(which was murdered in the same year), a pastoral
opera wrote by the Laureat, which the hydra-headed
multitude resolved to worry without hearing, a
custom with authors of merit, when Mrs. Raftor
came on in the part of Phillida, the monstrous roar
subsided," Chetwood has written. " A person in the
stage-box, next to my post [as prompter] called out
to his companion in the following elegant style—
' Zounds ! Tom ! take care, or this charming little
devil will save all ! ' " It must indeed have been an
exciting *première*.

Of the private life of Kitty Raftor since she came to
Drury Lane nothing is known, until her marriage is
recorded. Her husband was George Clive, a barrister
without practice, a brother of Sir Edward Clive, a
Baron of the Exchequer, and a second cousin of Robert,
Lord Clive.

The only reference to Clive is furnished by the
journalist, John Taylor : " He was a very learned and
intelligent man, by all accounts ; but without practice
in his profession ; he was therefore invited to become
the domestic companion of Mr. Ince, a gentleman
of fortune, and reputed to be the Templar in the club
of the *Spectator*. Mr. Ince was well known to be a
frequent contributor to that admirable periodical
work. My old friend, the Rev. Richard Penneck of the
British Museum, knew Mr. Ince, and told me that he
retained the practice, as mentioned in the *Spectator*,
of visiting the playhouse, almost every evening, as
long as his health and age would admit."

It has been said that the marriage took place in 1732. Percy Fitzgerald has called attention to the facts that on the playbill for October 3, 1733, when *Rule a Wife and Have a Wife* was performed, Miss Raftor was in the cast ; while two days later she was billed as " Mrs. Clive, formerly Miss Raftor." It is not unreasonable, he contends, to conclude that the marriage took place on the intervening day. Mr. Fitzgerald was, however, in error when he advanced as alternative theory : " We might have a suspicion that in the case of *mésalliance* as this, certainly Mr. Clive would not have been in such a hurry to have it so promptly announced to the world ; and it may be that this change of name was in consequence of the separation which speedily followed the marriage." But this is to leave out of the question Kitty, a dominant, even domineering, personality, and one of the last people in the world, one would think, to consent to be party to a clandestine marriage. Was she not, too, a " star," and even in the eighteenth century a theatrical " star " thought herself the equal of anyone, and better than most. But this admittedly is conjecture. The definite proof that the separation did not take place in 1733 is to be found in the fact that Henry Fielding in his " Epistle to Mrs. Clive," prefaced to his play [taken from the French of Regnard] *The Intriguing Chambermaid*, published in the following year, referred to her as a wife :

" MADAM,

  " If addresses of this nature (notwithstanding the base purposes to which they have been perverted) were originally intended to express the gratitude of the Author for some favour received, or to celebrate the merit of some particular friend ; I think you have a very just title to this.

" Dedications, and indeed most panegyrics, have been generally confined to persons in high life ; not that good qualities are so ; but as the praise which most authors bestow comes not from the heart, nor is the effect of their gratitude for past favours, but of their necessity of future, it is not as much their business to enquire who best deserves praise, as who can best pay for it. And thus we often see an Epistle crammed with such gross, false, and absurd flattery, as the poet ought to be ashamed of writing, and the patron of accepting.

" But while I hold the pen, it will be a maxim with me, that vice can never be too great to be lashed, nor virtue too obscure to be commended ; in other words, that satire can never rise too high, nor panegyric too low.

" It is your misfortune to bring the greatest genius for acting on the stage, at a time when the factions and divisions among the players have conspired with the folly, injustice, and barbarity of the town, to finish the ruin of the stage and sacrifice our own native entertainments to a wanton, affected fondness for foreign music ; and when our nobility seem eagerly to rival each other, in distinguishing themselves in favour of Italian theatres, and in neglect of our own.

" However, the few who have yet so much English taste and good-nature left, as sometimes to visit that stage where you exert your great abilities, never fail to receive you with the approbation you deserve ; nay, you extort, by the force of your merit, the applause of those who are languishing for the return of Cuzzoni. . . .

" But as great a favourite as you at present are with the audience, you would be much more so, were they acquainted with your private character ; could they see you laying out great part of the profits which arise to you from entertaining them so well, in the support of an aged father ; did they see you who can charm them on the stage with personating the foolish and vicious characters of your sex, acting in real life the part of the best wife, the best daughter, the best sister, and the best friend.

" The part you have maintained in the present dispute between the players and the patentees, is so full of honour, that had it been in higher life, it would have given you the reputation of the greatest heroine of the age. You looked on the cases of Mr. Highmore and Mr. Wilks with compassion, nor could any promises or views of interest sway you to desert them ; nor have you scrupled any fatigue (particularly the part which at so short a warning you undertook in this farce) to support the cause of those whom you imagined injured and distressed ; and for this you have been so far from endeavouring to exact an exorbitant reward from persons little able to afford it, though I have known you offer to act for nothing, rather than the patentees should be injured by the dismission of the audience.

" In short, if honour, good-nature, gratitude, and good sense, joined with the most entertaining humour, wherever they are found, are titles to public esteem, I think you may be sure of it ; at least, I am sure they will always recommend you to the sincere friendship of

  " Madam,

   " Your most obliged humble servant,

    " HENRY FIELDING."

When exactly the separation between Kitty Clive and her husband took place is immaterial : it was probably within a couple of years of the marriage. It would seem that it was mutually agreed, and it is more than likely that the ground was incompatibility of temperament. Kitty, always truculent when any cause of dispute arose, was probably " gey ill " to live with. Certainly there was no misconduct, anyhow on her part, for she was one of the few notable actresses of the eighteenth century whose character was without stain. When she was asked why she did not visit certain people of noble rank, whose private life was not irreproachable, she replied,"Why, because, my dear, I choose my company, as I do my fruit : therefore I am not for damaged quality."

Kitty Clive was not an easy person to have in the theatre, as presently David Garrick found to his cost. In 1736, it was proposed to revive at Drury Lane *The Beggar's Opera*. Whereupon a battle royal ensued—to the distress of the management, and the delight of everyone else. Kitty was the leading comedienne of the theatre, and naturally demanded the part of Polly Peachum, in which Lavinia Fenton had made so great a hit. Unfortunately, Susannah Cibber also wanted the part. Each enlisted all the influence she could, and the party feeling ran high. " No two women of high rank ever hated one another more unreservedly than these great dames of the theatre," Thomas Davis has written. " But though the passions of each were as lofty as those of the first Duchess [Lavinia Fenton married the third Duke of Bolton], yet each wanted the courtly art of concealing them." The Handel-Buonicini question, which divided all society from royalty downwards, was as nothing to this !

" When Mrs. Cibber was cast for Polly Peachum, she was very young [she was only six years junior to

Kitty], handsome, and an approved singer," Benjamin Victor, subsequently Treasurer of Drury Lane Theatre, and author of a useful theatrical history, wrote to Theophilus Cibber long after. " She had every requisite to make the best Polly that had ever appeared, and so had Mrs. Clive for Lucy : it would undoubtedly have been a fine entertainment so performed—but Clive was there in possession of the public voice—she was disgusted at the thought of leaving Polly, and lodged her complaint. What a storm was raised ! but their favourite, right or wrong, was to be supported, though against judgment and common sense. I remember I was one of your friends that advised you to give it up—your wife was then new to the stage, and the match was perfectly unequal, and so the only opportunity of seeing the *Beggar's Opera* in perfection was lost."

A ballad, in the strain of " Chevy Chase," dated January, 1737, appeared :

" Heaven prosper long our noble King,
    Our lives, and save us all ;
A woful quarrel lately did
    In Drury Lane befall.
To charm the pit with speech and song
    Dame Cibber took her way :
Players may rue who are unborn
    The quarrel of that day.
Cibber, the syren of the stage,
    A vow to heaven did make,
Full twenty nights in Polly's part
    She'd make the playhouse shake.
When as these tidings came to Clive,
    Fierce Amazonian dame :
' Who is it thus,' in rage she cries,
    ' Dares rob me of my claim ? '
With that she to the Green-room flew,
    Where Cibber meek she found ;
And sure if friends had not been by
    She had fell'd her to the ground."

"I find," says Fielding, speaking in the character of Susannah Cibber's husband, "that by our theatrical squabbles and altercations we make as much amusement to the town in a morning as by our performance in an evening. The contentions for the part of Polly between Mrs. Clive and my late—I was going to say wife—but a late woman who was called by many a name. That contest, I remark, furnished a copious topic for conversation, argument, and publication, and ended with noise and uproars in the playhouse. The consequence of all these addresses has been this: the town is called into the playhouse as the *dernier ressort*, to judge of things." It may be explained that Theophilus Cibber's first wife, Jenny Johnson, died in 1733, and that the following year he married Susannah Maria Arne, a sister of the composer. In 1738 he brought an action against her and one Sloper, claiming £5000 damages, but, it being proved that he had connived at the adultery, the jury awarded him £10!

Kitty Clive retained her popularity with the public, and, indeed, increased it as the years went on. Her one conspicuous failure was in *The Merchant of Venice* in 1741, when she played Portia to the Shylock of Charles Macklin. She burlesqued the part, to the joy of many spectators; but received severe rebukes from the critics.

At this time the actress received the following emoluments—the figures are taken from the salary-list of Drury Lane for the year 1742–43 : Salary, £15 15s. a week, certain, £525 ; clear Benefit, £200 ; clothes, £50 ; tickets at her Benefit, as per agent, £21 ; total £796. No inconsiderable sum in those days. But the theatre, now being financed by a wealthy amateur, Charles Fleetwood, was in a parlous financial condition, and the enterprise was only saved by the acquisition of David Garrick to the company—in the period referred to, he received, in all £1130. It was decided that as the expenses were too high, economies must be effected—and economy in the theatre means invariably the reduction of the salaries of the actors and actresses. This, Kitty Clive would not tolerate, and sturdily vented her grievance in a pamphlet (assuredly not written by her)—"The Case of Mrs. Clive *Submitted to the Public*"—a diminutive little pamphlet. It is well known that Kitty was deficient not only in style, but even in spelling : so it is not unlikely that she was aided in this venture by Fielding or some literary friend ; but the language is unmistakably hers, and there is one passage rather " Irish and less nice," which comes perilously near to being " a bull."

She began by saying bluntly, that the reason for her not acting that season was the advice of her friends. " Such appeals as the present," she went on to say, "were by some thought presuming and impertinent, but where injustice and oppression were concerned —this could never be a matter of indifference to the public—she appeals without affectation to her own claims on her regard of that public."

" I am the more encouraged to hope this from experience : it having been observed that these performers, who have had the happiness to please on the stage, and who never did anything to offend the public, when they have been injured by those who presided over theatres, have seldom, if ever, failed to redress upon representing the hardships they met with. If any think I treat this matter too seriously, I hope they will remember that, however trifling such things may appear to them, they are of

E

great importance, such as my liberty and livelihood depend on."

She then proceeds to explain the condition of the actors in reference to the managers. " They were quite helpless, as only two theatres were authorised, and the managers, connected together, complained of the actors' salaries being too great, and accordingly a false account was published in the daily paper—by whom I will not say. Whether or no some particular salaries were so, I will not pretend to determine. But whether the expense of the theatre was too high or otherwise, it was not the refusal that drove them to secede, but the tyranny of the two managers." She then dwells on her own particular hardship. When the revolters were obliged to return to their duty, she was offered by the manager of Drury Lane such terms as bore no proportion to what he gave other performers, or to those he had offered her at the beginning of the season. These she accordingly refused, and she applied to the other theatre— " for I knew it had been settled by some sort of agreement that part of the actors were to go to Covent Garden, and others to Drury Lane." Yet though Covent Gardens had before tempted her with high offers, and offered exactly the same terms she had found at Drury Lane, she was, however, persuaded to accept " some very little better," and had to submit a sum of money for her benefit, though she had enjoyed one clear of all expense for nine years before.

" When I was fixed at this theatre, I determined to stay there ; I did in all things which related to my profession, submit entirely to the manager's direction, and with the help of other principal performers, did greatly promote his interest, as was evident from the audiences, after we went to act there ; but I

found by his behaviour, it was designed I should not
continue with him, but return the next season to
Drury Lane.

" The agreements betwixt that manager and me
were verbal, but made before two gentlemen of
character and fortune, on whom I must depend for
the fulfilling of them : they were for one year. At
the end of the acting season, the manager sent an
office keeper to me with some salary that was due,
who required a receipt in full. I told him a very
great part of my agreement was yet due, and requested to see the manager, who came and acknowledged them, and promised to bring one of the gentlemen who was present at our engagements in a day
or two and pay me ; but he has not paid me," adds
Kitty in her downright style, " nor have I ever seen
him since, or as much as heard from him."

" It has always been a custom in theatres, that if
any actor or actress was to be discharged, or their
allowance lessened, they were acquainted with it at the
end of the season : the reason of this will appear to be
the giving them a proper notice to provide themselves.
This the manager of Covent Garden did to all his
company whom he designed to discharge, or whose
allowance was to be lessened, *except to me*, which made
me actually then conclude he determined I should
continue with him, till I was undeceived by his play
bills with the names of other actresses in parts I used
to perform. So that he has not only broke through
the customs of the theatre, but those in practice
almost everywhere, in dismissing me, and has done
me a real injury, in such an unprecedented act of
injustice. For had I been informed of this design
at the end of the season, I could have made terms to
have acted in *Ireland*, where I had met with most

uncommon civilities, and received very great advantages, which I shall ever remember with the utmost gratitude, and take this and every other opportunity to acknowledge. . . .

" It is pretended by the management that they have the same right to discharge an actor that a master has to turn away a servant, than which nothing can be more false and absurd : for when a master dismisses a servant there are many thousands besides to apply to, but when managers dismiss an actor, where are they to apply to ? It is unlawful to act anywhere but with them. Necessity or inclination brings every one to the stage : if the former happens to be the case, they will not readily find an employment; and if the latter they will not be fit for one, so that it will appear an act of great injustice and oppression. . . . But there is a very melancholy instance that the actor's demands is not the reason of dismissing them, but the will of the manager alone. Since last season an actor or actress returned to Drury Lane, under such abatements as that manager thought proper, and such as were in no degree equal to their merits and yet at the beginning of the season were dismissed after having been from their infancy on the stage and having no other profession to live by, and very numerous families to support.

" The manager of Drury Lane, though he can't but know I am disengaged from the other theatre, has not made any application to me to act with him, which he has done to several others who quitted that stage at the time I did. The reasons which obliged me to leave him still subsist. He owes me a hundred and fifty pounds, twelve shillings, which he acknowledged to be justly due, and promised payment of it by last Christmas to a person of too great consequence to mention here, the greater part of it (which ?) money I expended for clothes for his use. He offered me last season, not near half as much as he afterwards agreed to give another performer, and less than he gave to some others in his company, so that I must conclude that there is a design to distress me, and reduce me to such terms as I cannot comply with.

" I am sorry I am reduced to say anything in favour of myself : but I think I merit as much as another performer, and the managers are so desirous to convince me of the contrary, I hope I shall be excused, especially when I declare that at this time, I am not in the least vain of my profession.

" As to my performances, the audiences are the only and proper judges : but I may *venture to affirm that my labour and application have been greater than any other performer on the stage.* I have not only acted in almost all the plays, but in farces and musical entertainments ; and very frequently two parts in a night, even to the prejudice of my health. I have been at great expense in masters for singing : for which article alone the managers give five and six pounds a week. My additional expenses in belonging to the theatre amount to upwards of one hundred pounds a year in clothes and other necessaries ; and the pretended great salaries of ten and twelve pounds a week, which have been so artfully and falsely represented to the town, to the prejudice of the actors, will upon enquiry, appear to be no more than half as much ; since they performed last season, at the theatres, very seldom above three or four days a week.

" I have now finished all I proposed : I have shown in how aggravating a manner, without any reason assigned, I have been turned out of Covent Garden Theatre. The manager of Drury Lane, though he cannot but know what just reaons I had for quitting him, has never applied to me to return, nor made the least excuse for not paying my arrears.

" The reason of my taking the liberty to communicate these things to the public is most earnestly to intercede for their favour and protection, from whom I have always met with great generosity and indulgence. For, as I have always declared in a letter published by me last year in the daily papers, that I had not a fortune to support me independent of my profession. I doubt not, but it will appear I have made any considerable acquisition to it since, having not received two hundred pounds salary for acting in plays, farces, and singing : though other performers have received more than twice that sum. I have in consideration of these hardships been promised the protection of many ladies to whom I have the honour to be personally known, and will not doubt the concurrence of a public in receiving my performance in the best manner I am, at present, capable of, which I shall always gratefully acknowledge."—C. CLIVE.

There is mention about this time of her in the correspondence of Horace Walpole, who was to become an intimate friend of hers. He wrote to Horace Mann on May 26, 1742 : " There is a little simple farce at Drury Lane, called ' Miss Lucy in Town ' [partly written by Henry Fielding], in which Mrs. Clive mimics the Muscovita admirably, and John Beard, Amorevoli intolerably. But all the run is now after Garrick, a wine merchant, who is turned player, at Goodman's Fields. He plays all parts, and is a very good mimic. His acting I have seen, and say to you, who will not tell it again here, I see nothing wonderful in it ; but it is heresy to say so : the

Duke of Argyll says, he is superior to Betterton. Now I talk of players, tell Mr. Chute, that his friend Anne Bracegirdle breakfasted with me this morning. As she went out, and wanted her clogs, she turned to me, and said, " I remember at the playhouse, they used to call Mrs. Oldfield's chair, Mrs. [Elizabeth] Barry's clogs, and Mrs. Bracegirdle's pattens ! "

Kitty Clive would not give way, and during the next years acted and sang wherever she could. It was not until Garrick became manager of Drury Lane in 1747 that she returned to that theatre, where she remained until her retirement twenty-two years later. On her merits as a comedy actress every critic agreed. " Mrs. Porter in the vehemence of rage, and Mrs. Clive, in the sprightliness of humour, I have never seen equalled," Dr. Johnson remarked. " What Clive did best, she did better than Garrick ; but could not do half so many things. She was a better romp than any I ever saw in nature." Boswell has recorded : " Dr. Johnson used at one time to go occasionally to the Green-room of Drury Lane Theatre, where he was much regarded by the players, and was very easy and facetious with them. He had a very high opinion of Mrs. Clive's comic powers, and conversed more with her than with any of them. He said, ' Clive is a good thing to sit by ; she always understands what you say.' And she said of him, ' I love to sit by Dr. Johnson ; he always entertains me.' " As for Boswell, he just said : " Mrs. Clive was the best player I ever saw."

Fielding, who spoke with more authority, was scarcely less enthusiastic than Boswell. " Mrs. Clive is esteemed by all an excellent comic actress ; and as she has a prodigious fund of natural spirit and humour off the stage, she makes the most of the poet's on it," he said. " Nothing, though ever so barren, even though it exceeds the limits of nature, can be flat in her hands. She heightens all characters of humour she attempts ; nor is she confined only to the hoyden Miss or pert chambermaid, but in spiritous gay characters of high life, she always appears with such air, mien, and action, as speak the gay, lively, and desirable. She has been, by persons who remember both, compared to Mrs. Mountford ; and by their natural talents for the stage, I am apt to believe the comparison not unjust. I must, however, observe, Mrs. Mountford appeared with great success, *en Cavalier*, and made an adroit pretty fellow ; Mrs. Clive does not appear in these characters, the concealing petticoat better suiting her turn of make than the breeches. It is not from want of spirit or judgment to hit off the fop or the coxcomb, as she has evidently proved in the ballad she sings, called ' The Life of a Beau,' in which her action and gesture is as pleasing as in any part she performs. I could wish she would never attempt serious characters in comedy, and resign the part of Ophelia in *Hamlet*, in which she is is very unequal to herself. Yet all will allow, that ' take her all in all,' she has such talents as make her an excellent actress."

Even Charles Churchill succumbed to Kitty Clive's charm :

> " First giggling, plotting chambermaids arrive,
> Hoydens and romps, led on by General Clive.
> In spite of outward blemishes, she shone,
> For humour famed, and humour all her own.
> Easy, as if at home, the stage she trod,
> Nor sought the critic's praise, nor fear'd his nod :
> Original in spirit and in ease,
> She pleased by hiding all attempts to please :
> No comic actress ever yet could raise,
> On Humour's base, more merit or more praise."

If Kitty Clive had outstanding merit as an actress, she had her defects as member of a theatrical company. She could be, and generally was, delightful to general society, but more often than not she was a holy terror in the Green-room. Of her jealousy of the more popular Peg Woffington, something will be said in another chapter of this book. She was on terms of something like enmity with one of the leading actors, Henry Woodward. It is related by Tate Wilkinson that during the performance of *The Taming of the Shrew*, Woodward, exasperated, as he made his exit threw her down with such violence as to convince the audience that Petrucchio was not so lordly as he assumed to be. It is not surprising that the actress was so furious that " her talons, tongue, and passions were very expressive to the eyes of all beholders, and it was with the utmost difficulty that she suppressed her indignation." The next time the actress scored in the most dignified manner. " Mrs. Clive who, in *The Double Dealer*, performed Lady Froth," says Davies, " had by mistake, or in a hurry, laid on more rouge than usual, and *Brush, the valet*, played by Woodward, instead of saying ' Your coachman, having a red face,' said ' *Your Ladyship has a red face.*' This was no sooner uttered than peals of laughter were redoubled all over the theatre. Woodward affected to look abashed and confounded : Clive bore the incident heroically. When they were in the Green-room, the players expected a scene of altercation ; but the inimitable actress disappointed them. ' Come, Mr. Woodward,' she gravely said, ' let us rehearse the next scene, lest more blunders should fall out.' "

Kitty Clive for her benefit in 1761 chose a play translated from the French, *The Island of Slaves*.

Some one wrote to a newspaper, protesting that an English piece should have been selected. She assumed that this was the work of a colleague at Drury Lane, Edward Shuter, an excellent comedian, and she let fly. " I hope," she wrote in reply, " I may be indulged, though a woman, to say I have always despised the French Politics, but I have never yet heard we were at war with their wit : it should not be imputed to her, as a crime, to have a translation produced, when one part in three of all the comedies now acting are taken from the French, besides those of modern authors that have sneaked into the theatres without confessing from where they came." So far, so good ; but then her good angel deserted—or her adviser lost his head. " It does not seem, by the style of his letter," she went on to say, " that he is very intimately acquainted with his own language, but it is evident he knows nothing of French." Shuter, who subsequently swore an affidavit that he was not guilty of the attack, contented himself with printing a letter she had written to him :

" I Much Desire you would Do Me the Favour to let me know if you was the author of a letter in *The Dayle Gazeteer* relating to his New Piece I had for me benefet ; as it was intended to hurt my Benefet, and serve yours everybody will naturely conclude you was the author if you are not ashamed of being so I suppose you will own it : if you really was not concerned in wrightin it I shall be very glad : for I should be extreamly shock'd that an actor should be quilty of so base an action ; I dont often take the liberty of wrighting to the Publick but am Now under a Nessity of Doing it—therefore Desier your answer."

It was Garrick, however, upon whom fell the brunt

of her ill-temper, and her ill-temper became as the years passed more and more venomous. Tate Wilkinson says, " She knew every sore place in that sensitive being, and could make his withers wince whenever she pleased." Of her knowledge she took full advantage. It may be assumed that Garrick the man would have given her her congé, and that it was Garrick the manager, who, because of her drawing power, retained her as a member of his company. The following correspondence shows something of what he had to put up with.[1]

Catherine Clive to the Managers of Drury Lane Theatre
" *February* 13, 2 *o'clock*, 1768.

" GENTLEMEN,

" I am advised (I may say it is insisted in by my best friends) not to be a dupe of your ill-treatment of me, by giving up above half of my income at a time when I know I can have no alternative. I know it is in vain to expostulate with people in power : whether I am injured or not will appear to all who are *impartial :* as to your sneering me about my consequence, you may take what steps you please with your power, but you can't mortify me. It is *necessary* to explain one thing which may be convenient to be forgot by you, that when Mr. Lacy agreed with me in the summer he gave me his word that everything relating to my engagement this season should stand as it did in my last article, where my Benefit is *particularised* to be on or before the 17th of March ; of the truth of this I will take my oath. As to Mr. Woodward insisting upon having my day, he may insist on having part of my salary—I have nothing

---

[1] Since one specimen of her spelling has been given, the other letters have been modernised.

to do with him, and have behaved always to the managers of the play-house I belonged to, in an honest and open manner never having had *schemes* or designs to undermine or disappoint them in their business. Therefore whatever mine may be, you shall not have it to say I took the advantage of Mrs. Pritchard's illness to distress your plays. As to my Benefit you shall do as you please, as I have no written agreement."

David Garrick to Catherine Clive
"*Friday night, February* 14, 1768.

" DEAR MADAM,

" You always choose to have some quarrel at your benefit, and without reason ; but I do not. I am surprised that you have not thanked the managers for this kindness, instead of writing so peevish a letter. Your benefit is now settled upon the best day of the week, and six days sooner than you were last year. This was meant kindly for you, and every lady must see it in that light. I shall be sorry that you will not accept of that day (as you are pleased to say), because I wish you well, and it will be of great service to you : therefore if you will not advertise and fix your play, your folly be upon your own head. I cannot do more than I have done for you, and your friends must blame you."

Catherine Clive to the Managers of Drury Lane Theatre
"*Friday, February* 18, 1768.

" SIR,

" I am much surprised to hear that you have fixed the 17th of March for my Benefit, and that Mrs. Dancer is to have the Monday before (which as

Mr. Hopkins tells me was designed for Mr. Barry).
I hope I shall not be guilty of vanity in saying that
upon Drury Lane Theatre, neither Mr. Barry nor
Mrs. Dancer have a right to their benefits before me.
I have done you great service this season, and at
every call, when they either could not, or would not
play, have been the stop gap in playing principal
parts—and even when I have been extremely ill;
I do not suppose that expostulation will have any
effect to alter what you and the lady have been
pleased to settle. Therefore all I mean by giving
you this trouble, is to assure you I will not accept
of that day, nor will I advertise for it. If I am wrong
in this determination, I may lose my friends, and they
will naturally think you have acted honourably."

Catherine Clive to the Managers of Drury Lane Theatre
                              " *February* 19, 1768.
    " SIR,

        " I am sorry to give you this trouble, but I
really cannot comprehend what you mean by saying
you expected I should thank the managers for their
tenderness to me. I have always been grateful to
everyone who has obliged me, and if you will be so
good as to point out the obligations I have to you
and Mr. Lacy, I shall have great pleasure in acknow-
ledging them. You tell me you have done all you *can*
for me, and you *can* do *more*. I don't know how you
understand that. Any one who sees your letter would
suppose I was kept at your theatre out of charity.
If you still look over the number of times I have
played this season—you must think I have deserved
the money you give me. You say you give me the
best day in the week. I am sorry I cannot be of your
opinion. St. Patrick's Day is the very worst to me

that can be. Mrs. Yates' might be the strongest benefit, as her interest and mine clash in the Boxes. As to my *quaviling* you are under a very great mistake. There is nothing I dread so much; I have not spirits for that, though have for acting. You say that you have fixed the day, and have drawn a line under it that I may be sure I can have no other : therefore I must take it—But I must think it (and so will every impartial person) very hard that Mrs. Dancer should have her benefit before Mrs. Clive. You may depend upon having no further trouble with me. Indeed, I flattered myself that as the greatest part was past of the season, and I had done everything you asked of me, in playing a very insignificant part on purpose to please you, *I say*, I was in hopes it would have ended as it had gone so far, without any unkindness. But I shall say no more than that."

David Garrick to Catherine Clive

" Saturday, February 19, 1768.

" DEAR CLIVE,

" How can you be so ridiculous, and still so cross, to mistake every word of my letter, that I could have so low a thought as you suggest about *charity*, and which I am ashamed to read in yours. The *insignificant part* which you said you acted to oblige me, is very insignificant indeed as well as the piece it is in, so you have endeavoured to be rude to me without effect—you speak of these things, just as you are *in* or *out* of humour ; so it shall stand for nothing. However, I have such a regard for you for the future, you shall be no more troubled with any nonsense of mine, and I am rejoiced that you have cancelled the obligation you say you conferred upon me by accepting the part, by ungenteelly telling

me of it. You will find in your present humour
objections to any day; but we really meant you
kindly in giving you your own day, that you might
avoid opera nights, and have nobody to come immediately before or after you. This I did not do out
of *charity*; but out of that respect which I ever pay
to genius, and it is not my fault if Mrs. Clive will
not be as rational off the stage, as she is meritorious
on it."

Now and again, however, she was in the right.
Once, owing to the illness of a performer in another
play, *The Devil to Pay* was put on almost at the last
moment. Kitty was notified, but she was out of
town, and, though she came back as soon as possible,
she arrived too late. She was *fined!* Imagine—or
rather read—her indignation.

Catherine Clive to David Garrick

" I have great regret, in being obliged to say anything that looks like contention. I wish to be quiet
myself, and I am sure I never laid any scheme in my
life to make one any uneasy or unhappy. In regard
to the affair of *The Devil to Pay*, I sent in complaints
to the managers by the prompter, to beg that it might
not be done till the weather was cool, as the quickness
of the shift puts me in a flurry, which gives me a
violent swimming of the head. I beg you would do
me the favour to let me know if it was by your order
my money was stopped last Saturday. You was so
good indeed last week to bid me take *care*, or I
should be caught—I thought you were laughing, I
did not think it was a determined thing. It was never
before expected of a performer to be in waiting when
their names are not in the *papers* or *bills ;* the public

are witness for me whether I have ever neglected my business. You may (if you please to recollect) remember I have never disappointed you four times since you have been a manager; I always have had good health, and have ever been above subterfuge. I hope this stopping of money is not a French fashion; I believe you will not find any part of the English laws that will support this sort of treatment of an actress, who has a right, from her character and service on the stage, to expect some kind of respect. I have never received any favours from you or Mr. Lacy, nor shall ever ask any of you, therefore hope you will be so good to excuse me for endeavouring to defend myself from what I think an injury; it has been too often repeated to submit to it any longer. You stopped four days' salary when I went to Dublin, though you gave me leave to go before the house shut up, and said you would do without me. If I had known your intention, I would not have lost any of my salary, as my agreement with Mr. Barry did not begin till our house had shut up. I had my money last stopped at the beginning of the season for not coming to rehearse two parts that I could repeat in my sleep, and which must have cost two guineas, besides the pleasure of coming to town.

" When I was sent to, I recollected I had given my servant leave to go out, as I did not want her, who had the key of all my things : neither had I the necessary things ready if she had been at home. I had a friend's equipage come to me for Greenwich, to dine with them, and take my leave as they are going to Bath. I was very unhappy after I was there, and the gentleman was so obliging as to send one of his grooms at half-an-hour after four, to let you know I would come if you could not do without me. I had a carriage

CATHERINE CLIVE AS MRS. RIOT
By A. Mosley

ready with the horses put to, when he came back—
it wanted some minutes to six. It is very happy for
me that they happen to be people of consequence,
who know the truth of what I say, and who will be
very much surprised to hear how I have been
treated.

" I am sure I have always done everything in my
power to serve and oblige you : the first I have most
undoubtedly succeeded in : the latter I have always
been unfortunately unsuccessful in, though I have
taken infinite pains. I have never envied you your
equipage, nor grandeur, the fine fortune you have
already and must still be increasing. I have had
but a very little share of the public money. You
gave Mrs. Cibber £600 for playing sixty nights, and
£300 to me for playing 180, out of which I can make
it appear it cost me £100 in necessaries for the stage ;
sure you need not want to take anything from
it."

Yet even to her well-hated Garrick, she could be
generous. " One night," John Taylor has recorded,
" as Garrick was performing *King Lear*, she stood
behind the scenes to observe him, and in spite of the
roughness of her nature, was so deeply affected, that
she sobbed one minute and abused him the next,
and at length overcome by his pathetic touches,
she hurried from the place with the following
extraordinary tribute to the universality of his
powers, 'D—n him, I believe he could act a grid-
iron. ' "

Then, again, there is a letter from her to Garrick,
which he endorsed. " A love-letter—the first I
ever had from that truly great comedian, Mrs.
Clive."

F

Catherine Clive to David Garrick

" *November* 27, 1768.

" DEAR CLIVE,

   " I am most extremely obliged to you for your
very polite letter. How charming you can be when
you are good, I believe there is only one person in the
world who has never known the difference. I shall
certainly make use of the favour you offer me ; it
gives me a double pleasure—the entertainment my
friends will receive from your performance and the
being convinced that you have a sort of sneaking
kindness for your Pivy. I suppose I shall have you
tapping me on the shoulder (as you do to Violante)
when I bid you farewell, and desiring one tender look
before we part, though you may recollect and toss
the pancake into the cinders. You see I never
forget your good things. Pray make my best compliments to Mrs. Garrick, and believe I shall
always have sincere pleasure when I can assure
you,

   " I am, your obliged and humble servant,

                              D. GARRICK."

   In 1769, when she was fifty-eight, she decided to
retire from the stage. Garrick in vain urged her to
stay yet awhile. When he realised that her decision
was final, he placed himself at her disposal for her
last appearance on April 24—it was her benefit—
and played Don Felix to her Violante in *The Wonder*.
Also, *Lethe* was performed, in which she played Mrs.
Riot, the Fine Lady.

Catherine Clive to David Garrick

" *London, April* 14, 1769.

" DEAR SIR,

" I could not stay till the 24th to thank you
for your very kind letter. I am extremely glad to
hear you continue to be so well. I have often enquired after you of your brother George : now do
not say to yourself, ay, for your own sake, for when
I heard you were in such great pain, I was most
sincerely sorry. In the next place, to be sure I am
glad you are well for the sake of my audience, who will
have the pleasure to see their own Don Felix. What
signifies fifty-two ? they had rather see *the* Garrick
and *the* Clive at a hundred and four, than any of the
moderns ;—the ancients, you know, have always
been admired. I do assure you, I am at present in
such health and such spirits, that when I recollect
I am an old woman, I am astonished. My dear town
are giving me such applause every time they see me,
that I am in great fear for myself on my benefit night,
I shall be overcome with kindness. Indeed, I have
every day fresh instances of the public affection for
me. Lord Clive has behaved in a noble manner ; he
sent me the most polite note, and fifty pounds for his
box. I am greatly obliged to Sir William Stanhope :
if he should be at Bath when you receive this, I beg
you would do me the favour to return my thanks to
him ; I hope I shall have the pleasure of doing it at
Twickenham. You are very much mistaken if you
imagine I shall be sorry to hear Mr. Clive is well ;
I thank God I have no malice or hatred to any body :
besides it is so long ago since I thought he used me ill,

that I have quite forgot it. I am glad he is well and happy.

"Pray make my best respects to Mrs. Garrick, who I hope is so well as not to want the waters."

On the other hand, if to some of her colleagues she was troublesome, to Jane Pope Kitty Clive held out a helping hand, and, in fact, was at pains to instruct her in her work. Miss Pope was actually thirty-one years younger than the famous actress, and made her *début* at Christmas 1756 at the age of fourteen in Garrick's one-act entertainment *Lilliput* at Drury Lane. When *The Confederacy*, by Vanbrugh, was acted three years later, she played the part of Corinna. "I well remember," Tate Wilkinson has recorded, "on the second night of *The Confederacy*, Mrs. Clive called Miss Pope into the Green-room, before her going on the stage as Corinna, and said to her, ' My dear Pope, you played particularly well on Saturday as a young actress, but take from me a piece of advice, which I would have every performer attend to. You acted with great and deserved approbation, but to-night you must endeavour to act better, and to expect to receive less applause. The violent thunder of applause last Saturday, on your first appearance was not all deserved ; it was only benevolently bestowed to give you the pleasing information that they were well delighted, and had their warmest wishes that you would hereafter merit the kindness they bestowed upon you." Strangely enough, these words of wisdom were not taken amiss. Jane Pope remained at Drury Lane until 1775, when she lost her head, and quarrelled with Garrick about salary.

Jane Pope to David Garrick

> " *Wednesday, May* 31, 1775.

" Sir,

" The verbal agreement which passed between us three seasons ago is this year at an end. I should be glad to make a new engagement, and beg to know the terms you propose. I have, Sir, the honour to be

" Your most humble servant,

" J. POPE."

David Garrick to Jane Pope

" ADELPHI,

" *June* 3, 1775.

" The proprietors of the Theatre Royal in Drury-lane present their compliments to Miss Pope, and hope she has no objection to continue her engagement with them for three years or more, or as long as she pleases."

Jane Pope to David Garrick

" *Monday, June* 5, 1775.

" Miss Pope presents her respectful compliments to Mr. Garrick, or to the Proprietors of the Theatre Royal in Drury-lane; did not imagine they would have named a term of years without an addition of salary: as they are well assured of her dislike to change, and as she has never asked them any thing that has been unreasonable, she throws herself upon Mr. Garrick's or the Proprietors' generosity, to name what addition to her appointment they think her diligence deserves."

David Garrick to Jane Pope

" *Saturday, June* 9, 1775.

" Mr. Garrick's compliments to Miss Pope—his
brother's great danger for these four days has prevented his attending to any business.   The Patentees
sincerely wish that Miss Pope would have no objection
to continue her present agreement with them.   They
should be very sorry to lose her, and hope that they
may depend upon her being at Drury-lane for many
years to come.   Should Miss Pope be induced to quit
her present situation, they shall expect an answer in
the course of next week, as her place will be with
great difficulty supplied.   If they have no answer to
this, they shall depend upon her continuing with
them.   They not only acknowledge her diligence, but
her merit."

Jane Pope to David Garrick

" *Sunday, June* 10, 1775.

"Miss Pope presents her compliments to the Patentees, is very much honoured in their commendation,
both as to her merit and diligence, the former she
never thinks of, as she has been infinitely overpaid
by the public, who have ever shown her the greatest
favour, without even a paragraph to prejudice them.
Her diligence respects the managers, and from them
she looks for the reward due to it,—an equal portion
with others that rank in the same situation ;—can
assure them that such is her partiality for Drury-lane,
that she shall quit it with infinite regret, and it is their
fault alone that she is not there as long as her acting
powers shall subsist ; but she is determined at length
to shake all affection off, and like the Swiss to perform

only with those that pay best.   Her demand is ten
pounds per week, the sum usually paid to actresses
in her walk.   If the Patentees have any objection,
desires they may part in friendship, as she cannot
upon other terms remain at Drury-lane."

David Garrick to Jane Pope

"*June* 12, 1775.

" The Patentees with their best wishes to Miss
Pope, feel as much regret in losing her as she can
possibly do in quitting them.   Though they cannot
agree to the addition which she insists upon to her
present salary, they assure her that they part on the
terms of friendship she desires ;   they wish her every
happiness that her change of place and sentiments
can give her :   at the same time, they beg leave to
observe, that if Mr. Garrick would have agreed to let
Mrs. Barry perform Beatrice and Clorinda, and Mr.
Barry to have had his benefit the day which he gave
last year to Miss Pope, they should not have lost those
capital performers.   Mr. Garrick takes no merit to
himself in having done this, but that of showing a
little more than *Swiss attachment* to Miss Pope."

Jane Pope resigned almost at once.   However, she
expressed her regret, and asked to be taken back ;
but the actor-manager refused, until Kitty Clive intervened on behalf of her protégé.

Catherine Clive to David Garrick

" Now let me say one word about my poor unfortunate friend, Miss Pope, I know how much she dis-
obliged you, and if I had been in your place, I believe
I should have acted just as you did.   But by this time

I hope you have forgotten your resentment and will look upon her late behaviour, as having been taken with a dreadful fit of vanity, which for the time took her senses from her, and having been tutored by an affected heart, which helped to turn her head ; but recollect her in the other light, a faithful creature to you, on whom you could always depend, certainly a good actress, amiable in her character, both in being a very modest woman, and very good to her family, and to my certain knowledge has the greatest regard for you. Now my dear Mr. Garrick, I hope it is not yet too late to reinstate her before you quit your affairs here. I beg it ! I entreat it ! I shall look on it as the greatest favour you can confer on

> " Your ever obliged friend,
>> " C. CLIVE."

Churchill paid Jane Pope a pretty compliment in *The Rosciad* :

> " With all the native vigour of sixteen,
> Among the merry troup conspicuous seen,
> See lively Pope advance in jig and trip,
> Corinna, Cherry, Honeycomb, and Snip.

> " Not without art, but yet to nature true,
> She charms the town with humour just, yet new.
> Cheer'd by her promise we the less deplore
> The fatal time when Clive shall be no more."

Miss Pope's life was without stain. No man's mistress was she, in a day when an actress's morality was generally regarded as a negligible quantity. One love affair she had—that is to say, she lost her heart to Charles Holland, a clever actor, who, playing under Garrick, was scarified by Charles Churchill in "The Rosciad," for imitating his master :

" Next Holland came : with truly tragic stalk,
    He creeps, he flies—a hero should not walk.
    As if with Heaven he warr'd, his eager eyes
    Planted their batteries against the skies ;
    Attitude, action, air, pause, start, sigh, groan,
    He borrow'd, and made use of as his own,
    By fortune thrown on any other stage
    He might, perhaps, have pleased an easy age ;
    But now appears a copy, and no more,
    Of something better we have seen before.
    The actor who would build a solid fame,
    Must Imitation's servile arts disclaim ;
    Act from himself, on his own bottom stand ;
    I hate e'en Garrick thus at second-hand."

Holland was a vulgar, illiterate man ; but women
fell for him, because of his charm and good looks.
Miss Pope gave her heart, and never took it back—
she never cared for another. Yet she knew him treach-
erous. He made love to her—and a few days later,
driving to Kitty Clive's at Little Strawberry Hill, she
saw him in a boat—to quote Doran : " making a day
of it with that seductive piece of mischief, Mrs. Bad-
deley. Miss Pope had a ' pang of jealousy,' as she
admitted ; but doubtless she would have forgiven,
but for the fact that Holland, well aware how badly
he had behaved, when he saw her next at rehearsal,
assumed a haughty bearing. The young woman
uttered no word of reproach—but they never spoke
again except on the business of the theatre. ' I have
reason to know,' said the unhappy lady, ' that he
never was really happy.' " This story of her life
she confessed to James Smith, who, with his brother
Horace, wrote the famous *Rejected Addresses*. In
vain had Garrick warned her against " the wayward-
ness, instability, and recklessness " of the man. In her
later days, she lived for a time in Queen's Street, but

found the Freemasons too lively neighbours. " From the Tavern, on a summer's evening, when windows are perforce kept open, the sounds of ' Prosperity to the Deaf and Dumb Charity ! ' sent forth a corresponding clatter of glasses, which made everybody in Miss Pope's back drawing-room, fit objects of that benevolent institution." Thus James Smith, who again wrote of her when she had moved to Newman Street : " She sat quietly and calmly in an arm-chair by the fireside, patting the head of her poodle dog, and smiling at what passed in conversation, without being at all conscious of the meaning of what was uttered."

" Jane Pope had played as a child when Garrick was in the fullest of his powers," John Doran has written of her ; " won his regard, and the friendly counsel of Mrs. Clive ; played hoydens, chambermaids, and half-bred ladies, with a life, dark, and manner, free from all vulgarity ; laughed with free hilarity that begot hilarious laughing : and the only question about her was not if she were an excellent actress or not, but as an actress, in what she most excelled. She gave up young parts for old as age came on, and would have done it sooner, but that managers found her still attractive in the younger characters. In them, she had been without a rival ; and when she took to the Duennas and Mrs. Heidelbergs, she became equally without a rival," She retired on May 26, 1808, playing on that evening for the first and last time Deborah Dowlas in *The Heir-at-Law*. She survived for another ten years.

For many years before Kitty Clive retired she was a pet of Horace Walpole, who loved her audacity and her humour, and frequently invited her to Strawberry Hill. He even paid her the greatest compliment in his power and printed her Benefit cards. " Our dinner passed off very well," he wrote to George Montagu, another friend of the actress, on August 12, 1748. " The Clive was very good company. You know how much she admires the Rev. Dr. Thomas Ashton's preaching. She says she is always vastly good for two or three days after his sermons ; but by the time that Thursday comes all their effect is worn out. I never saw more decent behaviour than Mrs. Pritchard's, and I assure you even [her son] Mr. Treasurer [of Drury Lane Theatre] was far better than I expected."

Exactly when Walpole lent her—or let her—Little Strawberry Hill, between Strawberry Hill and Teddington cannot be said with any exactitude ; but it was probably shortly after 1750, for, " Have you any Mrs. Clive pulls down barns that intercept your prospect," he asked Henry Conway Seymour, November, 1752. Again in November, two years later, he told Richard Bentley : " My principal employ in this part of the world, except surveying my library, which has scarce anything but the painting to finish, and planting at Mrs. Clive's, whither I remove all my superabundancies. I have lately planted the green lane that leads from her garden to the common. ' Well,' said she, ' when it is done, what shall I call it ? ' ' Why,' said I, ' what would you call it but Drury Lane ? ' "

Again and again after this, there is mention of the actress in his letters.

July 5, 1758—to Richard Bentley. " Nothing is equal to the fashion of the village [Twickenham]. Mr. [John Henry] Müntz says we have more coaches than there are in half France. Mrs. Pritchard has bought Ragman's Castle, for which my Lord Litchfield could not agree. We shall be as celebrated as Baiæ or Tivoli ; and, if we have not such sonorous names as they boast, we have very famous people : Clive and Pritchard, actresses ; Samuel Scott and Thomas Hudson, painters ; my Lady Suffolk, famous in her time ; Mr. H——, the impudent lawyer that Tom Hervey wrote against ; Paul Whitehead, the poet ; Richard Owen Cambridge, the everything."

July 26, 1757—to John Chute. " You never saw anything so droll as Mrs. Clive's countenance, between the heat of the summer, the pride in her legacy [of £50 left her by John Robartes, the last Earl of Radnor of that family], and her efforts to appear unconcerned."

January 14, 1760—to George Montagu. " I had a much more agreeable supper last night at Mrs. Clive's with Miss West, my niece Chomley, and Arthur Murphy, the writing actor, who is very company, and two or three more. Mrs. Chomondeley is very lively ; you know how entertaining the Clive is, and Miss West is an absolute original."

July 14, 1761—to Henry Seymour Conway. " All the morning I play with my workmen or animals, go regularly every evening to the meadows with Mrs. Clive, wait on with my Lady Suffolk, and at night scribble my ' Painters '—what a journal to send you. I carried my Lady Townshend, Lady Hertford, Anne Conolly, my Lady Hervey, and Mrs. Clive to my deputy's house at the gate of Westminster Hall. [To see the Coronation.] "

May 25, 1766—to George Montagu. " My Lady Shelburne has taken a house here, and it has produced a *bon mot* from Mrs. Clive. You know my Lady Suffolk is deaf, and I have talked much of a charming old passion, Madame du Deffand, who is *blind*. ' Well,' said the Clive, ' if the new Countess is but *lame*, I shall have no chance of ever seeing you.' "

December 25, 1770—to Henry Seymour Conway. " My cascades give themselves the airs of cataracts, and Mrs. Clive looks like the sun rising out of the ocean. Poor Mr. Raftor is tired to death of their solitude, and as his passion is walking, he talks with rapture of the brave row of lamps all along the street, just as I used formerly to think no trees beautiful without lamps to them, like those at Vauxhall."

June 29, 1777—to the Countess of Upper Ossory. " My Lady Townshend, in the days of her wit, said that Mrs. Clive's face rose on Strawberry Hill, and made it sultry ; but, I assure you, you may sit now in her beams when she is in her zenith without being tanned."

June, 1778—to the Countess of Upper Ossory. "Poor Mrs. Clive has been robbed again in her own lane, as she was last year, and has got the jaundice, she thinks, with the fright. I don't make a visit without a blunderbuss, so one might as well be invaded by the French."

February 1, 1779—to the Countess of Upper Ossory. " Half I have said I know is heresy, but fashion had gone to excess, though very rarely with so much reason. Applause had turned Garrick's head, and yet he was never content even with that prodigality. His jealousy and envy were unbounded ; he hated Mrs. Clive, till she quitted the stage, and then cried her up to the skies, to depress Mrs. Abington. He did not love Mrs. Pritchard, and with more reason, for there was more spirit and originality in her Beatrice than in his Benedict."

Kitty Clive was as truculent at Little Strawberry Hill —Walpole christened it Clive's-den—as at Drury Lane. " I remember a reply which she made to two very decent respectful men, then in office as surveyors of the roads in the parish, on my father's sending them to her, as being the acting magistrate of the place, to demand some payment which she had refused : it was in the laconic terms, ' By the living G——, I will not pay it,' Miss Hawkins has related. ' I suppose this might destroy entirely all intercourse with our house, for she was of course compelled to break her oath. I suppose it was to show " what some actresses *can* do—what some *will* do," that she worked for the Holbein chamber at Strawberry-hill, the carpet with blue tulips and yellow foliage.'

" Mrs. Clive, the comic actress, I believe, by her agreeable or rather diverting society paid rent for what is called little Strawberry-hill. Her memory still survives in the place ; and her bounty to her indigent relations, is recorded on a tablet affixed to the wall of the church. A virtue less known, and perhaps less easily credited, considering her manners in private, and her cast of characters in public, was her perfect abstinence from spirituous liquors. She told a lady, her neighbour, in Great Queen Street, Lincoln's Inn Fields, from whom I had it, that she believed she could say more than most players could, that she never kept any of these exhilarating resources in her house.

" When one of her maid-servants, to whom she had given an admission to see her act, was asked how she liked her mistress on the stage, she said ' *she saw no difference between her there and at home.*' It is most probable from this, that the character in which she had seen her, was Nell in the farce of *The Devil to Pay*.

" I have heard it said that she once attempted Shylock, and with the Jewish accent, but the effect was too ludicrous to be endured.

" Mrs. Clive visited my father and mother, but on my mother's running out of the house one evening, when she called accidentally, to prevent her alighting from her carriage, as the small-pox had made its appearance amongst us, and she knew Mrs. Clive not to have had it—utterly insensible to the politeness of her attention at a moment of such anxiety, she roughly replied, ' It was not you I wanted to see, it was your husband : *send him out !* ' "

The actress's correspondence was typical of her, though how she, taking her lack of education into consideration, came to write such good letters it is difficult to imagine. It may be that they were written from dictation by her brother James—usually referred to—and addressed as " Jemmy." He had followed her into retirement, and they were devoted to each other. He was an exceptionally bad actor, but a pleasant enough man ; and Walpole liked him. " Raftor has left the stage," he says in 1770. " Mrs. Clive has very kindly taken him to live entirely with her, and I hear he is exceptionally happy at it."

Catherine Clive to George Colman

" *April* 12, 1771.

" Sir,

" I hope you heard that I sent my servant to town to inquire how you did ; indeed I have been greatly surprised and sincerely concerned for your unexpected distress, there is nothing can be said upon these melancholy occasions to a person of understanding. Fools cannot feel, people of sense

must, and will, and when they have sunk their spirits
till they are ill, will find that nothing but submission
can give any consolation to inevitable misfortunes.
I shall be extremely glad to see you, and think it
would be right, if you would come and dine here two
or three days in a week, it will change the scene, and
by the sincerity of your welcome, you may fancy
yourself at home."

Catherine Clive to David Garrick

[?, 1772.]

" I screamed at your parish business. I think I see
you in your churchwardenship quarrelling for not
making those brown loaves big enough ; but for
God's sake never think of being a justice of the peace,
for the people will quarrel on purpose to be brought
before you to hear you talk, so that you may have as
much business upon the lawn, as you had upon the
boards. If I should live to be thawed, I will come to
town on purpose to kiss you ; and in the summer,
as you say, I hope we shall see each other ten times
as often, when we will talk, and dance, and sing, and
send our hearers laughing to their beds.

> " ' O jealousy thou raging pain,
> Where shall I find my peace again.'

"I am in a great fuss. Pray what is the meaning
of a quarter of a hundred of the Miss Mores coming
purring about you with their poems, and plays, and
romances ; what, is the Pivy to be roused, and I
don't understand it. Mrs. Garrick has been so good
to say she would spare me a little corner of your heart,
and I can tell the Miss Mores they shall not have one
morsel of it. *What!* do they pretend to take it by
force of lines? If that's the case I shall write such

verses as shall make them stare again, and send them
to Bristol with a flea in their ear ! Here have I two
letters, one and not one line, nay, you write to the
poulterer's woman rather than the Pivy, and order her
to bring me the note ; and the poor creature is so
proud of a letter from you, that it has quite turned
her head, and instead of picking her poultry ; she
is dancing about her shop, with a wisp of straw in her
hand, like the poor Ophelia, singing :

" ' How should I true love know.'

And I must tell you, if you don't write to me directly
and tell me a great deal of news, I believe I shall sing
the next of the mad songs myself. I see your run
always goes on, which gives me great pleasure—I
shall be glad if you will lend it me (Colley Cibber) ;
my love to my dear Mrs. Garrick. I suppose you had
a long letter of thanks from Miss Pope. I have had
one from her all over transport. I feel vast happiness
about that affair, and shall ever remember it as a
great obligation you have conferred on your,

"PIVY CLIVE."

David Garrick to Catherine Clive

" HAMPTON,

" *Friday Morning.*

" MY DEAR PIVY,

" Had not the nasty bile, which so often con-
fines me, and has heretofore tormented you, kept me
at home, I should have been at your feet three days
ago. If your heart (somewhat combustible like my
own) has played off all the quibs and rockets which
lately occasioned a little cracking and bouncing

G

about me, and can receive again the more gentle and pleasing firework of love and friendship, I will be with you at six this evening to revive by the help of those spirits in your tea-kettle lamp, the flame which was almost blown out by the flouncing of your petti-coat when my name was mentioned.

"'Tea is a sovereign balm for wounded love.'

"Will you permit me to try the poet's recipe this evening? Can my Pivy know so little of me to think that I prefer the clack of Lords and Ladies to the enjoyment of humour and genius? I reverence most sincerely your friend and neighbour, not because he is the son of one of the first of our ministers, but because he is himself one of the first ministers of literature. In short, your misconception about that fatal *champatra* (the devil take the word!) has made me so cross about everything that belongs to it, that I curse all squibs, crackers, rockets, air-balloons, mines, serpents, and Catherine-wheels, and can think of nothing and wish for nothing but laugh, gig, humour, fun, pun, conundrum, carriwitchet, and Catherine Clive!

"I am ever Pivy's most constant and loving, etc.,

"D. GARRICK.

"My wife sends her love and will attend the cere-mony this evening."

Catherine Clive to David Garrick

"TWICKENHAM,

"*January* 13, 1774.

"DEAR SIR,

"I should suppose, when you see Twickenham, you will not presently imagine whom the letter can come from, you have so entirely forgot me.   I write because I am importuned by the bearer; and to solicit a great man looks as if one had power, which, you know, is a charming thing.   Mr. Crofts tells me he knows you well : he lives at Twickenham, is a wine merchant, lives in good credit, and has for many years.   I have taken my wine of him these four years, which is the reason *he thinks* I ought to trouble you with a letter.   He wants to get his son into the excise. He tells me you are at the head of the commission, and can do whatever you please : *you could, I know, in former days ;* and if you can now, and *will*, Mr. Crofts will be very glad of it.   I do not know anything of the young man, therefore cannot recommend him, but I suppose his father *can*, for he is a fine chatterbox, he *will be up and tell you* everything about him.

" Pray how does my dear Mrs. Garrick do ? for I will love her, because I am sure she would me, if you would let her.

" I might date this letter from the Ark ; we are so surrounded with water that it is impossible for any carriage to come to me, or for me to stir out, so that at present my heavenly place is a little devilish.   I believe I must win a house in the Adelphi, and come to town in winter : but when I come I shall not have the happiness to see Macklin in *Macbeth*.   What a pity it is he should make an end of himself in such a *fine part*.

" Your friend Jemmy and Mrs. Mestiver desire their compliments to yourself and Mrs. Garrick, I suppose we shall all meet next summer at Mr. Walpole's."

Catherine Clive to David Garrick

" TWICKENHAM,

" *January* 23, 1774.

" WONDERFUL SIR,

" Who has been for thirty years contradicting an old-established proverb, ' you cannot make bricks without straw '; but you have done what is infinitely more difficult, for you have made actors and actresses without genius, that is, you have made them pass for *such*, which has answered your end, though it has given you infinite trouble. You never took much pains with yourself, for you could not help acting well; therefore I do not think you have much merit in that, though to be sure it has been very assuaging to yourself, as well as the rest of the world ; for while you are laughing at your own conceits, you were at the same time sure they would cram your iron chests. What put the fancy in my head, was your desiring a good character of young Crofts. It is a sad thing an exciseman cannot get his bread unless he has behaved well in the world ; and yet it is perfectly right, that everybody would have the same caution, not to give good characters when they did not deserve them, not receive people into your family for servants, or any kind of business, who had them not. If this was made an unalterable rule, the world must in time become *all* sorts of good people.

" I send the enclosed which may be depended on. Mr. Costard is our rector, one of the most learned and best sort of men in the world. They say he has more knowledge of the stars, and among the sky-people than anybody, so that most of us take him for a conjuror. I ought to make an apology for being so troublesome, when I come to town I will make my excuse, when I shall at the same time see Mrs. Garrick, which will always be a real pleasure to dear sir,

"Yours,

"C. Pivy."

Catherine Clive to David Garrick

"TWICKENHAM,

"*March 22, 1775.*

"There is no such being now as Pivy: she has been killed by the cruelty of Garrick; but the Clive thank God is still alive, and alive like to be, and did intend to call you to give an account for your wicked wishes to her. But having been told of your good deeds and great acting events, I concluded you were in too much conceit with yourself to listen to my complaints. I must needs say that I admire you with the rest of the world, for your great goodness to Miss Hannah More: the protection you gave her play. I daresay she was sensible you were of the greatest service to her; she was sure everything you touched would turn into gold, and though she had great merit in her writing, still your affection for tragedy children was a great happiness to *her*, for you dandled it and fondled it, and then carried it in your arms to town.

"I must now mention the noblest action of your life, your generosity to nephew David; all the world is repeating your praises. The people who always envied you and wished to detract from you, always declaring you loved money too much, ever to part from it, now they will *feel* foolish, and look contemptible: all that I can say is, *I wish that heaven had made me such an uncle.*

"I hope dear Mrs. Garrick is perfectly well; happy she must ever be; she has a disposition which will make her so in all situations. You and I, you know, can alter our tempers with the weathercock. We are all here at present but queer. Mrs. Mestiver is not sick (but sorry); your Jemsey is neither one thing nor the other—always dreaming of Garrick and the opera.

"Everybody is raving against Mr. Sheridan for his supineness. The country is very dull: we have not twenty people in the village, but still it is better than London. Let me see you—let me hear from you: and tell me all the news you can to divert your ever affectionate and forgiving

"C. Clive.

"Our brother and sister join in compliments to your lady and self."

Catherine Clive to David Garrick

"Twickenham,

"*June* 23, 1776.

"Dear Sir,

"Is it really true that you have put an end to the glory of Drury Lane Theatre?[1] *If it is so*, let me congratulate my dear Mr. and Mrs. Garrick on their approaching happiness: *I know* what it will be, you cannot yet have an idea of it; *but* if you should still be so wicked not to be satisfied with that *unbounded*, uncommon degree of fame you have received as an actor, and which no other actor ever did receive—

---

[1] Garrick appeared on the stage for the last time on June 10, 1776.

nor no other actor ever *can* receive,—I say, if you should still long to be dipping your fingers in their theatrical pudding (now without plums), you will be no Garrick for the Pivy. In the height of public admiration for you, when you were never mentioned with any other appellation but Mr. Garrick, the charming man, the fine fellow, the delightful creature, both by men and ladies; when they were admiring everything you did and everything you scribbled, at this time *The Pivy* was a living witness that they did not know, nor could they be sensible of half your perfections. I have seen you with the magical hammer in your hand, endeavouring to beat your ideas into the heads of creatures who had none of their own. I have seen you with lamb-like patience, endeavouring to make them comprehend you, and I have seen you when that could not be done. I have seen your lamb turned into a lion; by this your great labour and pains the public was entertained; they thought they all acted very fine—they did not see you pull the wires.

"There are people now on the stage to whom you gave their consequence, they think themselves very great, now let them go on in their new parts without your leading strings, and they will soon convince the world what this genius is. I have always said this to everybody, even when your horses and mine were in their highest prancing. While I was under your control I did not say half the fine things I thought of you, because it looked like flattering, and you know your Pivy was always proud, besides I thought you did not like me then, but now I am sure you do, which made me send this letter."

Jane Pope to Catherine Clive

" MONDAY, *February* 22, 1779.

" DEAR MADAM,

" I have attempted several times to sit down and answer your very kind letter, and have as often been interrupted, but at length I am determined you must know I never think of writing but when I fancy I have some novelty to relate, and at present only one theme obtains, which is respecting the admirals. This always ends in breaking the windows.

"I am much mortified you did not spend Ash Wednesday with us, as the whole party, I believe, sincerely expected it, and would have been glad to see you : the Roffeys came to town on purpose, and inquired after you immediately. Miss Griffith spent the day with Miss Cadogan, like another Niobe, and so romantic, it is astonishing : I believe love is at the bottom with both of them, for that seems the most natural ; however, they say you are vastly affected, and that you all wept the other morning like the ladies in *The Funeral*, and Mr. Raftor came in like Counsellor Puzzle to fill up the group. I wish I could give you something to laugh at, for I do not think weeping becoming to you or to me : at least it should be seldom. . . . What reason you have to applaud yourself for your conduct : every comfort and every hour to enjoy, convince me you were right, and I pray heartily I may tread in your steps (at least in some degree) to share such a portion of happiness. I am tired with subscriptions, for (I am sorry to say it) worthless people ; yet did not one contribute, one would be considered a Barbarian. They are setting on foot something of that sort for Mrs. Bellamy, who

is, I hear, starving; she has wearied everybody with
her letters, and is penniless, without food, fire, or
candle—in short nothing can be more wretched :
and I should not be surprised if some ladies in the
theatre, who now carry their heads very high, were
reduced sometime or other, to the same state."

Catherine Clive to Jane Pope

" TWICKENHAM,

" *October* 17, 1784.

" MY DEAR POPY,

" The jack I must have, and I suppose the cook
will be as much delighted with it as a fine lady with
a birthday suit. I send you walnuts which are fine;
but pray be moderate in your admiration, for they are
dangerous dainties. John has carried about to my
neighbours above six thousand, and he tells me there
are as many still left; indeed, it is a most wonderful
tree. Mrs. Prince has been robbed at two o'clock, at
noon, of her gold watch and four guineas, and at the
same time our two justices of sixpence a-piece; they
had like to be shot, for not having more. Everybody
enquires after you, and I deliver your compts. Poor
Mrs. Hart is dead—well spoken of by everybody. I
pity the poor old Weasel that is left behind.

" The jack must carry six or seven and twenty
pounds, the waterman shall bring the money when I
know what."

For Kitty Clive's latest years, Walpole is the
principal authority.

" I did not see the Clive last night," he wrote to
Earl Harcourt on May 18, 1781, " as she was gone to

Mrs. Franks's, but I left your Lordship's invitation with Mrs. Mestiver, who told me that her sister was very weak and out of order, and so I find by the enclosed, which I received this morning. Indeed, poor women, they are both in a bad way ! "

The actress was now usually in ill-health. " Pray tell Lord Harcourt," he wrote to the Rev. William Mason in August, 1782, " that poor Clive is better, yet her fits of jaundice return so often that I fear her recovery. Indeed, the apothecary fears her liver is affected—she is shrunk to an extraordinary degree." In the same month he told the Countess of Upper Ossory that " Clive's-den is little less than an infirmary"; and the Earl of Strafford, that "Mrs. Clive is certainly very declining, but has been better of late ; and, which I am glad of, thinks herself better." To Earl Harcourt he wrote early in the next month : " Dames, Old dowagers : she is so much recovered that she ventures to go out cruising on all the neighbours, and has made a miraculous draught of fishes."

In October, 1782, Walpole wrote again to the same correspondent : " Mrs. Cliveden, I flatter myself is really recovered, having had no relapse since I mentioned her last. She even partakes of the diversions of the carnival, which at Twickenham begins at Michaelmas, and lasts as long as there are four persons to make a pool. I am to go to her this evening to what she calls *only two tables*. I have preached against hot rooms ; but the devil, who can conceal himself in a black ace as well as in an apple or a guinea, has been too mighty for me, and so, like other divines, when I cannot root out vice, I join in it."

Kitty Clive died at Little Strawberry Hill on December 6, 1785, and was buried in Twickenham Churchyard. Horace Walpole put up an urn in the shrubbery attached to her cottage, with an inscription written by himself :

> " Ye smiles and jests, still hover round ;
> This is mirth's consecrated ground.
> Here lived the laughter-loving dame,
> A matchless actress, Clive her name ;
> The comic muse with her retired,
> And shed a tear when she expired."

HANNAH PRITCHARD (*née* VAUGHAN)
1711–1768

HANNAH PRITCHARD
(*née* VAUGHAN)
1711-1768

HANNAH PRITCHARD attained to a conspicuous position in the theatrical world, and managers, the few there then, were for many years at her feet. Audiences were delighted rather than enraptured with her, but she never experienced the enthusiasm that was evoked by a Clive or a Woffington. Certainly, outside the four walls of the theatre, she was never in any way conspicuous. Even Knight, most enthusiastic and learned writer of dramatic biographies, has done little more in his account of Hannah Pritchard than give a list of the parts, though he emphasises her merits as an actress.

Of the personal history of Hannah Vaughan, as she was christened, little is known, beyond the facts that she was born in 1711 and in early life married an actor called Pritchard. Of him even less is known, though he certainly lived for many years, since he was given a benefit at Drury Lane in 1747. It is also on record that, when Hannah was two-and-twenty she played the part of Loveit in an opera, *A Cure for Covetousness, or, The Cheats of Scapin*, at Fielding and Hippisley's booth, Bartholomew Fair. As an intelligent critic pointed out, she was intended for better things, or, to quote his own phrase, of which no doubt he was inordinately vain, " a transportation to a brighter stage."

This acceptable " transportation " took place very soon—though it was as an actress, and not as a singer. In September of the year in which she made her debut she joined the company of " Comedians of His Majesty's Revels " at the Haymarket, the majority of whom had in consequence of disputes with the management, seceded from Drury Lane.

On the first night that the seceders opened the Haymarket, September 26, 1733, with *Love for Love*, Mrs. Pritchard played Nell in the after-piece, *The Devil to Pay*. Dr. Doran has written : "*The Daily Post* had already extolled the ' dawning excellence ' she had exhibited in a booth, and prophesied that she would charm the world. She played light comic parts throughout the season, but her powers as a tragedian do not seem to have been suspected. Mrs. Pritchard thus entered on her long and honourable career, a married woman, with a large family, and an excellent character, which she never tarnished." It must be assumed that she was at once successful, for during the season she played several important parts, and created more than one character in newly produced plays. Among the rôles assigned to her at this period were, Dorcas in *The Mock Doctor*, Edging in *The Careless Husband*, Cleora in Fielding's *Opera of Operas, or, Tom Thumb the Great*, Sylvia in *The Double Gallant*, and Ophelia—a sufficiently wide range to test an actress's versatility. Indeed, with so little experience, it is really remarkable, even with adequate coaching, she can have done so well.

The seceders, having made up their differences with the managers of Drury Lane, returned to that theatre in the spring of 1734, and with them went Hannah

HANNAH PRITCHARD
By Hayman

Pritchard. There at this time, she generally, though not invariably, played comedy rôles. She was cast, among other parts, for Lady Wouldbe in *Volpone*, Belinda in *The Old Bachelor*, Lady Anne, Duchess of York in *Richard III*, Lady Macduff, Anne Boleyn, Desdemona, Rosalind, Viola in *Twelfth Night*, and Nerissa in *The Merchant of Venice*; and to her was entrusted the responsible task of creating Dorothea (to the Maria of Kitty Clive) in Miller's *Man of Taste*, and Peggy in Robert Dodsley's *The King and the Miller of Mansfield*.

Hannah Pritchard, on New Year's Day, 1742, made her first appearance at Covent Garden as Arabella in Ravenscroft's *The London Cuckolds*. In the following year she was back again at Drury Lane, where she was the original Clarinda in Henry Fielding's *The Wedding Day*.

The following items concerning her appear in the salary-list of that theatre for the season 1742–1743.

Salary, £7 10s. certain	. . . .	£250
Clear profit	. . . . .	180
Clothes	. . . . . .	50
		£480

In 1744 she went again to Covent Garden, and was entrusted with a large number of important parts during her three years' stay there. During this period she created Constance in Colley Cibber's *Papal Tyranny in the Reign of King John*—what a title for a play !—Tag in Garrick's *Miss in her Teens*, and Clarinda in Hoadley's *The Suspicious Husband*.

When Hannah Pritchard first met Garrick is not known, but no doubt—the dramatic fraternity being then a small body—it was soon after he came to London. Anyhow, in 1746, they were playing to-

H

gether in Shakespearian and other plays. In that year Richard Cumberland, then a scholar in the sixth form of Westminster School witnessed a performance of Rowe's *The Fair Penitent* in November 1746. Quin was Horatio ; Ryan, Altamont ; Mrs. Cibber, Calista ; and Mrs. Pritchard, Lavinia. Of the last mentioned he noted, " She was an actress of a different cast than Mrs. Cibber, had more nature, and, of course, more change of tone and variety both of action and expression : in my opinion, the comparison was decidedly in her favour."

Garrick must have been pleased with Hannah Pritchard's performance in his *Miss in her Teens*, for when he joined Lacy in management at Drury Lane in 1747, he invited her to leave Covent Garden, and join his company as a " star."

This is not the place to trace Mrs. Pritchard's theatrical career in detail ; but it must be mentioned that she created Irene in Dr. Johnson's *Mahomet and Irene*, on February 6, 1749. " In this, as first produced, Irene was strangled on the stage," Joseph Knight has recorded. " Audiences that accepted the suffocation scene in *Othello* need not, perhaps, have been expected to be more sensitive with regard to the bowstring in *Irene*. The audience, on the first night of *Mahomet and Irene*, shouted ' Murder,' and Mrs. Pritchard, unable to finish the scene, retired from the stage. The termination was altered, but Johnson seems never to have forgiven a woman he associated with his misfortune." Garrick, before the production, had suggested certain alterations, but the irascible author would have none of them. Revised, the play ran nine nights, when the author's three nights brought him £195, and he sold the copyright for £100 to Dodsley, the bookseller playwright. It is recorded that when he was asked how he felt the failure, he replied, " Like a monument." Anyhow, this decided him that his forte was not dramatic composition— and, indeed, it was not. As regards the actress, Johnson remarked : " Pritchard, in common life, was a vulgar idiot ; she would talk of her *gownd* ; but when she appeared upon the stage, seemed to be inspired with gentility and understanding." Again : " It is wonderful how little mind she has. . . . She was a very good actress ; but she had something affected in her manner : I imagine she had some player of the former age in her eye, which occasioned it."

Charles Churchill, on the other hand, lavished upon her in *The Rosciad* unstinted praise :

" Pritchard, by Nature for the stage design'd,
In person graceful, and in sense refined ;
Her art as much as Nature's friend became,
Her voice as free from blemish as her fame,
Who knows so well in majesty to please
Attemper'd with the graceful charm of ease ?
    When, Congreve's favoured pantomime[1] to grace,
She comes a captive queen, of Moorish race ;
With love, hate, jealousy, despair, and rage
With wildest tumults in her breast engage,
Still equal to herself is Zara seen ;
Her passions are the passions of a queen.
    When she to murder whets the timorous Thane[2]
I feel ambition rush through every vein ;
Persuasion hangs upon her daring tongue,
My heart grows flint, and every nerve's new strung.
    In comedy—Nay, there, cries Critic, hold ;
Pritchard's for comedy too fat and old :
Who can, with patience, bear the gray coquette,
Or force a laugh with over-grown Julett ?[3]
Her speech, look, action, humour, all are just,
But then, her age and figure give disgust.

                    .   .   .

[1] *The Morning Bride.*   [2] Macbeth.
[3] Juletta, a witty maidservant in *The Pilgrim.*

> Oft have I, Pritchard, seen thy wondrous skill,
> Confess'd thee great, but find thee greater still ;
> That worth, which shone in scatter'd rays before,
> Collected now, breaks forth with double power.
> ' The Jealous Wife ! ' on that thy trophies raise,
> Inferior only to the author's praise."

Life, then as now, was not all beer and skittles for
an actor-manager, as the following letter from David
Garrick to Mr. Pritchard shows.

" *July 11th*, 1747.

" SIR,

" I returned from Lichfield last night, and
found your letter upon the table. I am obliged to
you for the concern you express to Mr. Draper about
me, and he would have answered you, had I not been
here to do it myself. I was taken ill at Coventry with
a very sorry throat, caught, as I imagine, by lying in
damp sheets at Dunstable, but by an immediate bleed-
ing, purging, etc., etc., etc., I am now perfectly recovered and *in statu quo*. I am very sorry any of
your friends (if they really are such) trouble you with
letters of that sort you have sent me in abstract, nor
do I well know the reason of your sending it to me :
that Mr. Rich may be uneasy you have left him is very
natural ; but that any of these artifices should disturb your quiet (as you are well versed in theatrical
policy), surprises me much. Whatever proofs your
letter-writer may pretend to give you of my *partial
opinion* to any body else, I appeal to yourself whether
or no the bias of my actions has not inclined to your
family : I have dealt by you as one of my *own* family,
and I think your situation, with regard to me should
dispel suspicions and uneasiness.

" I have not engaged Mrs. Cibber as yet, and if I
should, you may depend upon it that no such stupid

article as playing with her [solely] shall be part of
the agreement. If you will consider the falsehood,
you may know that such clauses are incompatible
with my interest and inclination, and I am sorry they
should be thrown out to spoil the harmony I intend
shall subsist in our company.

" Mrs. Pritchard may depend upon the strictest
justice to the best of my judgment : nor shall it be
in the power of any haughty woman to injure her,
nor can I apprehend what is meant by that impudent
insinuation of deceiving you by appearances. It is
my interest (putting friendship out of the case), that
your wife should maintain her character upon the
stage ; if she does not, shall not the managers be
great losers ? I have employed my power to fix *you*
in the best station I could, and what I think will put
you upon the footing you should desire ; have I done
this, Sir, do you think, to deceive you with appearances ? or to show you my opinion of you, and inclination to you ? I am sorry I have occasion to say this
much, because I thought we were settled together in
such a manner, that no artifices or suspicions could
disconcert us. I have a great stake, Mr. Pritchard,
and must endeavour to secure my property and my
friends to the best of my judgment. I shall engage
the best company in England if I can, and think it
the interest of the best actors to be together : I shall,
to the best of my ability, do justice to all, and I hope
Mr. Pritchard and his friends will be the last to im-
peach my conduct, or be uneasy that I should follow
the bent of my judgment in my future management
of the stage. I do not find that there is at present
much talk about the theatre ; however, I flatter
myself (and on good reasons) that the world will not
think you have acted wrong by your engaging with

us, and that you run as little risk of ill treatment
from the present managers as from your former : however, if you have any doubts about you, and you had
rather choose Covent Garden than Drury-lane, let me
know it immediately (the very next post), and I will
do my endeavours with Mr. Lacy (for I will not let
him know it till then), to discharge you from any
agreement that may make you and Mrs. Pritchard
uneasy. I am just come from the house ; we are in the
midst of alterations and mortar, so you must excuse
this scrawl. Pray my best service to your wife and
all friends ; let me know your mind (for I am vexed a
little), and you shall hear from me soon again."

Hannah Pritchard acted regularly with Garrick
until her retirement. In 1767 she created her last
part, Mrs. Mayrick, the heroine in Kenneth's *The
Widowed Wife ;* and during the season of 1767 she
gave a series of farewell performances. " The house
was moved more deeply still on an after night—the
twenty-fourth of April, 1768—the night of Mrs.
Pritchard's final farewell," Doran has written, " when
Garrick played Macbeth in a brown court suit, laced
with gold, and she the ' lady ' with a terrific power
and effect such as even the audiences in those days
were little accustomed to. Her ' Give *me* the daggers '
on that night was as grand as her ' Are you a man ? '
and when the curtain descended, such another intellectual treat was not looked for in that generation."
On that evening she delivered a poetical address
written by Garrick, in which she says,

> " In acted passion tears must seem to flow,
> But I have that within that passeth show."

The actress, who was in her fifty-eighth year, left
the stage at the height of her fame and popularity.

The immediate cause for this move was, no
ill-health, for she at once went to Bath, where ——
died in the following August. A monument to her
memory was placed in Poet's Corner in Westminster
Abbey.

Writing of Hannah Pritchard when she retired,
John Doran, than whom no writer has more soundly
delved into the theatrical annals of the eighteenth
century, said of her, that it was even a more serious
loss to the stage than that of Susannah Maria Cibber.
He added :—

" She had well earned repose, after thirty-five years
of most arduous labour. In 1733, Mrs. Pritchard, a
young and well-respected married woman, was acting
at our suburban fairs ; but how much younger, as
Miss Vaughan, does not appear. Her slender cultivation, or, rather, her total want of education, is no
proof that she was not of a respectable family ; and
the pertinacity of her brother, a clever low comedian,
Henry Vaughan, in pursuing a claim to property left
by a relation, Mr. Leonard of Lyon's Inn, shows that
there was one quality connected with the family
which the world respects.

" Mrs. Pritchard did not at once win, but long
worked for, her fortune. Her husband held a sub-
ordinate post in the theatre, until her talents raised
him above it. Her history, in one point, resembles
Betterton's : it was a life of pure honest, unceasing
labour. She was too busy to afford much material
for further record. In another point it resembled
Mrs. Betterton's, in the unobtrusive virtue of her
character. While Margaret Woffington was pretending to lament on the temptations to which she yielded,
and George Anne Bellamy yielded without lamenting,
honest Mrs. Pritchard neither yielded nor lamented.

It is true that she was not so inexpressibly beautiful as Margaret, nor as saucily seductive as George Anne; but she carried with her the lustre of rectitude, and the beauty of honesty and truth. Living, she was welcomed wherever virtue kept home; and dying, she left fairly-acquired wealth, a good example, and an irreproachable name to her children.

" At first she fought her way very slowly, but played everything from Nell to Ophelia; and throughout her career she originated every variety of character, from Selima in *Zara*, to Tag in *Miss in her Teens;* from Mrs. Beverley in *The Gamester*, to Clarinda in *The Wedding Day;* from Hecuba to Mrs. Oakley.

" We are so familiar with the prints of her as Hermione and Lady Macbeth, and to hear of her awful power in the latter, as well as the force and dignity of her Merope, Creusa, and Zara; her almost too loud excess of grief in Volumnia, and the absolute perfection of her two queens, Katherine and Gertrude; that we are apt to remember her as a tragedian only. Her closet scene, as the Queen in *Hamlet*, was so fine and finished in every detail, that its unequalled excellence remains a tradition of the stage, like the Ophelia of Mrs. Cibber. There was a slight tendency to rant—[Garrick, on the other hand, put it, ' She was apt to blubber her grief ']—and some lack of grace in her style, which, according to others, marred her tragedy. There is no dispute, however, as to her excellence in comedy, particularly before she grew stout; and indeed, in spite of her becoming so, as in Millamont, in which, even in her latest years, her easy manner of speaking and action charmed her audience, though elegance of form and the beauty of youth were no longer there.

" As a perfectly natural actress, she was admirable

HANNAH PRITCHARD AS HERMIONE IN "A WINTER'S TALE"
After Pine

in such parts as Mrs. Oakley, Doll Common, and the
Termagant in *The Squire of Alsatia*. With such
characters she identifies herself. I find her less commended in artificial ladies like Clarissa ; for queens
of fashion, like Lady Townly and Lady Betty
Modish. Yet, although she only pleased in these
high-bred personages, she was ' unimitably charming '
in Rosalind and Beatrix, in Estifania and Clarinda,
in Mrs. Sullen and Lady Brute, and in all characters
of intrigue, gaiety, wit, playfulness, and diversity of
humour. I may sum up all by repeating that her
distinguishing qualities were natural expression, un-
embarrassed deportment, propriety of action, and an
appropriateness of delivery which was the despair of
all her contemporaries, for she took care of her con-
sonants, and was so exact in her articulations, that,
however voluble her enunciation, the audience never
lost a syllable of it. Mrs. Pritchard and Mrs. Abington
were selected, at various periods, to represent the
Comic Muse, and nothing can better illustrate this
quality and merit."

Mrs. Pritchard, who led a blameless life, died fairly
well off, thanks largely to a legacy from a distant
relation. It has been said, however, that she was
considerably bled by her brother, Henry Vaughan, who
was also on the stage. Of her marriage, there was
issue : one son and one daughter. The son was, it is
thought, for some time Treasurer of Drury Lane
Theatre. Of the daughter, more is known. She was
extraordinarily pretty, and, when she expressed a
desire to go on the stage, Garrick, much attracted by
her, himself coached her. She made her debut at
Drury Lane on October 9, 1756, as Juliet, to the
Romeo of Garrick, her mother playing Lady Capulet.
She scored an immediate success. After she played

many of Mrs. Pritchard's parts, including Betty Modish in *The Careless Husband*, Miranda, and Perdita, and she was entrusted with the creation of Harriot in Colman's *The Jealous Wife*, and Fanny in Garrick and Colman's *The Clandestine Marriage*. She retired at the same time as her mother. About six years earlier, she had married John Palmer, commonly known as " Gentleman Palmer "—an actor who must not be confused with the better-known John Palmer (1742–1798). Miss Pritchard's husband died in 1768, aged forty, his death being due to having inadvertently taken a wrong medicine.

CHARLOTTE CHARKE (*née* CIBBER)
DIED 1760

CHARLOTTE CHARKE (*née* CIBBER)
DIED 1760

IN the Introduction to *A Narrative of the Life of Mrs. Charlotte Charke, youngest daughter of Colley Cibber, Esq., Written by Herself*, which was published in 1775, it is written : " If no otherwise instructive, her Life will serve to show what very strange creatures *may* exist, and the endless diversity of habits, tastes and inclinations, which may spring up spontaneously, like weeds, in the hot-bed of corrupt civilisation." That the lady had a nice sense of humour is evident from the following address :

The Author to Herself.

" MADAM,

" Though flattery is universally known to be the spring from which dedications frequently flow, I hope I shall escape that odium so justly thrown on poetical petitioners, notwithstanding my attempt to illustrate those wonderful qualifications by which you have so eminently distinguished yourself, and gives you a just claim to the title of a nonpariel of the age.

" That thoughtless ease (so peculiar to yourself) with which you have run through many strange and unaccountable vicissitudes of fortune, is an undeniable proof of the native indolent sweetness of your temper. With what fortitude of mind have you vanquished sorrow, with the fond imagination and promissory hopes (only from yourself) of a succession of happiness, neither within your power or view ?

"Your exquisite taste in building must not be omitted : the magnificent airy castles, for which you daily drew out plans without foundation, must, could they have been distinguishable to sight, long ere this have darkened all the lower world, nor can you be matched, in oddity of fame, by any but that celebrated knight-errant of the moon, George Alexander Stevens, whose memoirs, and yours conjoined, would make great figures in history, and might justly claim a right to be transmitted to posterity ; as you are, without exception, two of the greatest curiosities that ever were the incentive to the most profound astonishment.

"My choice of you, Madam, to patronise my works, is an evident proof that I am not disinterested in that point, as the world will easily be convinced, from your natural partiality to all I have hitherto produced, that you will tenderly overlook their errors, and, to the utmost of your power, endeavour to magnify their merits. If, by your approbation, the world may be persuaded into a tolerable opinion of my labours, I shall, for the novelty-sake, venture for once to call you friend—a name, I own, I never as yet have known you by.

"I hope, dear Madam, as Manly says in *The Provoked Husband*, that ' last reproach has struck you,' and, that you and I may ripen our acquaintance into a perfect knowledge of each other, that may establish a lasting and social friendship between us.

"Your two friends, prudence and reflection, I am informed, have lately ventured to pay you a visit ; for which I heartily congratulate you, as nothing can possibly be more joyous to the heart than the return of absent friends, after a long and painful peregrination.

" Permit me, Madam, to subscribe myself for the future, what I ought to have been some years ago,

" Your real friend and humble servant,
" CHARLOTTE CHARKE."

The date of the birth of Charlotte Cibber is not known; but as she went on the stage in 1730, when she was quite young, the reader can guess for himself. She was the youngest child, " born at a time my mother began to think, without the additional blessing (meaning my sweet self) being just forty-five years of age when she produced her last, ' though not least in love.' " " I came," she has told us, " as an unexpected and unwelcome guest into the family," for since her mother had borne no children for some years, she was regarded as an intruder in the family circle. Her mother, however, loved her dearly, and her father saw to it that she had not only a genteel, but a liberal education, which, being intelligent, she was able to profit by. " I must beg leave to add," she admits, " that I was never much acquainted with that necessary utensil which forms the housewifery part of a young lady's education, called a needle, which I handle with the same clumsy awkwardness a monkey does a kitten, and am equally capable of using the one as pug is of nursing the other."

The spirit of mimicry awoke in Charlotte early, and she relates an incident that occurred when she was four years old :

" Having even then a passionate fondness for a periwig, I crawled out of bed one summer's morning at Twickenham, where my father had part of a house and gardens for the season, and taking it into my small pate, that by dint of a wig and waistcoat, I should be the perfect representative of my sire, I crept softly into the servants' hall, where I had the night before espied all things in order, to perpetrate the happy design I had framed for the next morning's expedition. Accordingly I paddled downstairs, taking with me my shoes, stockings, and little dimity coat, which I artfully contrived to pin up, as well as I could, to supply the want of a pair of breeches. By the help of a long broom, I took down a waistcoat of my brother's, and an enormous tie-wig of my father's, which entirely enclosed my head and body, with the knots of the ties thumping my little heels, as I marched along with slow and solemn pace. The covert of hair in which I was concealed, with the weight of a monstrous belt and large silver-hilted sword, that I could scarce drag along, was a vast impediment in my procession : and what still added to the other inconveniencies I laboured under, was whelming myself under one of my father's large beaver hats, laden with lace as thick and as broad as a brickbat.

" Being thus accoutred, I began to consider that it would be impossible for me to pass for Mr. Cibber in girl's shoes, therefore took an opportunity to slip out of doors after the gardener, who went to his work, and rolled myself into a dry ditch, which was deep as I was high, and, in this grotesque pigmy state, walked up and down the ditch bowing to all who came by me. But, behold, the oddity of my appearance soon assembled a crowd about me, which yielded me no small joy, as I conceived their risibility on this occasion to be marks of approbation, and walked myself into a fever, in the happy thought of being taken for the squire.

" When the family arose, till which time I had

CHARLOTTE CHARKE
After Gravelot

employed myself in this regular march in my ditch, I was the first thing enquired after, and missed, till Mrs. Heron, the mother of the celebrated actress of that name, happily espied me, and directly called forth the whole family to be witnesses of my state and dignity.

" The drollery of my figure rendered it impossible, assisted by the fondness of both father and mother, to be angry with me ; but, alas ! I was borne off on the footman's shoulders to my shame and disgrace, and forced into my proper habiliments."

Colley Cibber sent his youngest daughter, when she was eight years of age, to a well-known and highly regarded school in Park Street, Westminster, kept by a Mrs. Draper. The master of languages there was a Mr. Flahaut, who took a particular interest in the little girl, and persuaded her mother to let him teach her Latin and Italian, as well as French. Also he instructed her in geography—" which, by the way," she comments, " though I know it to be a most useful and pleasing science, I cannot think it was altogether necessary." However, she goes on to say : " I am delighted at being thought a learned person, therefore readily acquiesced with my preceptor's proposal. Accordingly, I was furnished with proper books, and two globes, celestial and terrestrial, borrowed of my mother's own brother, the late John Shore, Esq., sergeant-trumpet of England ; and pored over them until I had like to have been as mad as my uncle, who has given a most demonstrative proof of his being so for many years." She was also taught music and dancing.

When Charlotte's education was completed, she joined her mother at Hillingdon, near Uxbridge, which her father rented for a term of years. She took

I

quickly to a country life, and lived much in the open air, becoming an excellent shot and horsewoman. Presently, she, with the utmost audacity, and a nice sense of humour, set up a dispensary. " I summoned all the old women in the parish to repair to me whenever they found themselves indisposed. I was indeed of the opinion of Leander in *The Mock Doctor*, that a few physical hard words would be necessary to establish my reputation; and accordingly had recourse to a Latin dictionary, and soon gathered up as many fragments as served to confound their senses, and bring them into a high opinion of my skill in the medical science. As my advice and remedies, for all disorders were designed as acts of charity, it is not to be imagined what a concourse of both sexes were my constant attendants; though I own, I have been often obliged to refer myself to Salmon, Culpepper, and other books I had for that purpose, before I was able to make a proper application, or indeed arrive at any knowledge of their maladies. But this defect was not discovered by my patients, as I put on significancy of countenance that rather served to convince them of my incomparable skill and abilities." She was, indeed, spoiled to the top of her bent by her mother.

It was while at Hillingdon that Charlotte met Richard Charke, a minor member of the Drury Lane company, and promptly fell in love with him. She was modest enough later to attribute his interest in her, not to her charms, but to the fact that she was the daughter of Colley Cibber, who would probably help him to put his affairs, which were in a desperate state, into order. Her father gave his consent to the engagement. The marriage took place at St. Martin's-in-the-Fields in February—the year is believed to be

1729—but it was almost from the first unsatisfactory.

"I thought at that time the measure of my happiness was full, and of an ever-during nature," she writes, "But, alas! I soon found myself deceived in that fond conceit; for we were both so young and indiscreet, we ought rather to have been sent to school than to church, in regard to any qualifications on either side, towards rendering the marriage state comfortable to one another. To be sure, I thought it gave me an air of more consequence to be called Mrs. Charke, than Miss Charlotte; and my spouse, on his part, I believe, thought it a fine feather in his cap to be Mr. Cibber's son-in-law: which indeed it would have proved, had he been skilful enough to have managed his cards rightly, as my father was greatly inclined to be his friend, and endeavoured to promote his interest amongst people of quality and fashion. His merit as a proficient in music, I believe incontestible; and being tolerably agreeable in his person, both concurred to render him the general admiration of those sort of ladies, who, regardless of their reputation, make them the unhappy sacrifices to every pleasing object: which, *entre nous*, was a most horrible bar to my escutcheon of content, insomuch that married bliss was, the first twelvemonth of her connubial state, industriously employed in the pursuit of fresh sorrow, by tracing her spouse from morn to eve through the hundreds of Drury."

Charlotte was at pains to defend her action in leaving her husband. "As I have, among other censures, laboured under that of being a giddy indiscreet wife," she writes, "I must take this opportunity of referring myself to the superior judgment of those who read my story, whether a young creature, who actually married for love (at least I thought so; nay, was foolish enough to think myself equally beloved) must not naturally be incensed, when, in less than a month after marriage, I received the most demonstrative proofs of disregard, where I ought to have found the greatest tenderness : to be even to my face apparently convinced of his insatiate fondness for a plurality of common wretches, they were to be had for half a crown. This consequently raised in me both aversion and contempt; and, not having years enough to afford me reflection, nor patience sufficient to sit down, like Lady Easy, contented with my wrongs, till experience might by chance have made him wiser." However, presently, Charke, a worthless fellow, went to Jamaica, where he died twenty months later. "There seems to have been a touch of insanity, certainly there was no power of self-control in this poor woman," Doran has written. "From her childhood, she had been wild, wayward, and rebellious; self-taught, as a boy might be, and with nothing feminine in her character or pursuits. With self-assertion, too, she was weak enough to be won by a knave with a sweet voice, whose cruel treatment drove his intractable wife to the stage, where she failed to profit by her fine opportunities."

After Charlotte's partial separation from her husband —he called on her whenever he was hard up, in the hope that she would help him—she decided to go on the stage—a course that was not for her very difficult, owing to the position her father held in the theatrical world. Her first appearance was at Drury Lane, when she played Mademoiselle in *The Provoked Husband*, for the benefit of Mrs. Thurmond, on April 8, 1730. Twenty days later, she played the same part on the night when Nance Oldfield gave her last performance.

Mrs. Charke quickly made a name for herself—though she never became one of the great "stars." However, the audiences liked her, and she became, to a certain extent, a popular favourite. Owing to an accident to Mrs. Porter, she took that lady's part, Alicia in *Jane Shore*. Besides this, in the season of 1730–1731, she played Arabella in *The Fair Quaker*, and created Lucy in *George Barnwell* and Thalia in Cooke's *Triumph of Love and Honour*.

She was now, she mentions with pride, singled out from the rest of the company to be "stock-reader" to the theatre, in case of disasters—that is to say, she understudied all the female parts, and was supposed to be ready to take the place of anyone who was prevented from appearing—a sufficiently arduous task, for the undertaking of which her salary was raised from twenty to thirty shillings a week. Also there were perquisites. For instance, when Mrs. Butler was ill, Charlotte appeared in her place as the Queen in *Essex*. "In justice to the deceased gentlewoman," she says, "I must inform the reader she rewarded me for, by sending me, in a very polite manner, a couple of guineas next morning. I must needs say, I did not think it worth so handsome an acknowledgment ; but she sent it in such a manner that, had I refused it, I must have been guilty of a very great absurdity, as her station and mine at that time were upon very different footings ; I being but a babe in the business, and she an established person of a very good salary."

Not long after, one Hughes Highmore purchased Drury Lane, and she and her brother and others of the company went to the theatre in the Haymarket, where she earned so much as three pounds a week. She returned to Drury Lane, when it was under the management of Charles Fleetwood; but in 1735 had a dispute about parts, and, as she admits, "without the least patience or consideration, took a French leave of him, and was idle enough to conceive I had done a very meritorious thing. I cannot say, in the affair, he used me entirely well, because he broke his word with me; but I used myself much worse in the main by leaving him, as I have since experienced. As there are too many meddlers in the world, who are ever ready to clinch the nail of sedition, when once 'tis struck, so some particular people thought it worth while, by villainous falsehoods, to blow the spark of fire between Mr. Fleetwood and myself into a barbarous blaze, insomuch that I was provoked to write a farce on the occasion, entitled *The Art of Management*, wherein the reader may be assured I took no small pains to set him in a most ridiculous light, and spared not to utter some truths which I am sensible ought rather to have been concealed: and I cannot but own, I have since felt some secret compunction on that score; as he, notwithstanding my impertinent and stupid revenge, at my father's request restored me to my former station." Fleetwood, it is recorded, bought up the entire edition of the splenetic piece.

Charlotte Charke discourses of her domestic affairs about this period. "At the time I was engaged with Henry Fielding at the Haymarket, where he was running his play, *Pasquin*, I lodged in Oxendon Street, near Leicester Square, and boarded with my sister Brett, who was but an inmate as well as myself; but I and my little daughter swelled up the number of her family. I, being a sort of creature that was regarded as a favourite cat or mischievous monkey about the house, was easily put off with what reasonable people might have deemed not only an inconvenience, but an affront ; I accordingly was put into the worst apartment, and was entirely insensible of its oddity, until a blustering night roused me into an observation of its extraordinary delicacy. When I had thoroughly surveyed it, I sat down and wrote the following description of the room and exact inventory of my chattels :

" Good people for a while give ear
    Till I've describ'd my furniture :
With my stately room I shall begin,
    Which a part of Noah's ark has been :
My windows reach from pole to pole ;
    Strangely airy—that in winter, O my soul,
With the dear delight, of—here and there a hole.

" There is a chest of drawers too, I think,
    Which seems a trough, where pigeons drink ;
A handkerchief and naps as much as they'll contain :
    O ! but I keep no gowns—so need not to complain.

" Then, for my fire ; I've an inch of stove,
    Which I often grieve I cannot move
When I travel from the chimney to the door,
    Which are miles full three, if not fourscore.

" By that time, I, shiv'ring, arrive,
    I doubtful grow if I'm alive.
Two foreign screens I have, in lieu
    Of tongs and poker—nay, faith, shovel too.

" Sometimes they serve to fan the fire,
    For 'tis seldom that to bellows I aspire.
I'll challenge, England's King and the Pretender,
    To say, that e'er I rust my fender.

" That fashion's old, I've got a newer,
    And prudently make use of iron skewer.
Now for my lovely bed, of verdant hue,
    Which, ere Adam liv'd, might possibly be new.

" So charming thin, the darns so neat
With great conveniency expel the heat :
But these things will not ever last ;
Each day a curtain, in breathing, waste.

" Then, for chairs ; I indeed have one ;
But, since ruin draws so swiftly on,
Will let my room, ere chair, screens,
And curtains all are gone."

Leaving the stage, Mrs. Charke indulged in a series of the most fantastic adventures. She took it into her head " to dive into trade " ; rented a shop in Long Acre, and turned oil-woman and grocer—no doubt to the great amusement of her friends, and, to do her justice, of herself :

" This new whim proved very successful, for every soul of my acquaintance, of which I have a numerous share, came in turn to see my mercantile face, which carried in it as conceited an air of trade as it had before in physic, and I talked of myself and other dealers, as I was pleased to term it. The rise and fall of sugars were my constant topic ; and trading abroad and at home, was as frequent in my mouth as my meals. To complete the ridiculous scene, I constantly took in the papers, to see how matters went at Bear quay; what ships were come in, or lost; who in our trade was broke ; or who advertised teas at the lowest prices : ending with a comment upon those dealers who were endeavouring to undersell us ; shrewdly prognosticating their never being quiet, till they had rendered the article of tea a mere drug ; and that I and many more of the business should be obliged entirely to give up. An injury to traffic in general ! that must be allowed.

" I must beg leave, gentle reader, to tell you, that my stock perhaps did not exceed ten or a dozen

pounds at a time of each sort; but that furnished
me with as much discourse as if I had the whole lading
of a ship in my shop. Then as to oils, to be sure, the
famous Nobs and fifty more were not to be put in
competition with mine for their excellence; and
though I seldom kept above a gallon of a sort in the
house, I carried on the farce so far as to write to
country chapmen to deal with me.

"Then I considered, until I had established a
universal trade, I'd save, for the first year, the expense of an out-rider, as I was a very good horsewoman, and go the journies myself; concluding
with a significant nod, that money was as well in my
own pocket as another's. But, providentially for
me, I could gain no country customers, for, as the
case stood, I must positively let them have the goods
considerably to my own loss: and, as a proof, will
relate a circumstance that occurred to me in the
selling a quarter of a hundred of lump sugar to a
good-natured friend, who came to buy it, for no other
reason, but that I sold it.

"'Tis customary in buying sugars by the hundred,
to be allowed a tret of six pounds extra. I was so
insufferably proud of hearing so large a quantity
demanded by my friend, that I really forgot the character of grocer, and, fancying myself the sugar baker,
allowed in the twenty-five pounds the half of what
I got in the hundred; alleging that 'twas our way,
when people dealt for large quantities, to make an
allowance over and above the common weight.

"My friend, who knew no better than myself,
promised me all the custom she could bring, which,
if she had been as good as her word, might in due
course of time have paved the way for me either to
Newgate, the Fleet, or Marshalsea.

"After my friend had gone with her bargain, I began, as I thought trade increasing, to think it proper to purchase a large pair of scales to weigh by hundreds, and a large beam to hang them on; and set out next morning to that purpose, traversing through Drury Lane, Holborn, Fleet ditch, etc., but meeting with nothing to my mind, returned home, with a resolution to have a pair made.

"The good woman who kept the house, upon hearing I had been endeavouring to make this needless purchase, made bold to enquire into the necessity of it: upon which I told her what had happened the day before, and mentioned, as a proof of my knowledge of trade, the advantage I allowed to my friend. She for sometime left me amazed at her meaning, while she almost strangled with laughing at my folly.

"When she came to herself, I gravely asked where the joke lay, and what mighty wonder there was in my having an increasing trade, who had such an universal acquaintance? As soon as she was able to convince me of the error I had committed, in giving one half of the over-weight in a quarter of a hundred which was allowed in a whole hundred only, I began to drop my jaw, and looked as foolish as any reasonable person may suppose, on so ridiculous an occasion.

"Links and flambeaux are a commodity belonging to the oil trade, at least generally sold in shops of that kind, and constant and large demands I had for both: but, I remember, in particular, one of those nocturnal illuminators, who are the necessary conductors for those who did not choose chairs or coaches, came every night just before candle time, which is the dusky part of the evening, the most convenient light for perpetrating a wicked intent, as will be proved by the sequel.

" To be sure, I thought myself infinitely obliged to the sooty-coloured youth for using my shop, and was mighty proud of his handsel every evening ; and sometimes, as I dealt in spirituous liquors, treated him with a dram, and many thanks for his own and other gentlemen's custom of his profession. The arch villain smiled, and expressed great satisfaction that even, in his poor way, he had the power of serving his good mistress. He bowed and I curtseyed ; till, walking backwards out of my shop, he had complimented me out of every brass weight I had in it.

" He had not gone five minutes, ere I had occasion to make use of some of them ; when to my great amazement and confusion, not one was to be found. Unluckily for me, they were piled up one with the other, and injudiciously placed in the corner of the window next the door, quite pat to his purpose ; and he was really so perfect a master of his art in filching, that, notwithstanding the great ceremony that passed between us from the upper end of the shop to the lower, he went off entirely undiscovered in his villainy.

" I need not tell the reader 'twas the last interview we ever had, till I, to his great misfortune, saw him making a small tour in a two-wheeled coach from Newgate to Tyburn ; a college where many industrious squires like himself, have frequently and deservedly taken their degrees."

Later, Charlotte set up a puppet-show over the Tennis Court, in James Street, Haymarket, and at this time " was addressed by a worthy gentleman (being then a widow) and closely pursued till I consented to an honourable, though very secret alliance ; and in compliance to the person, bound myself by all the vows sincerest friendship could inspire never to confess who he was.   Gratitude was my motive to consent to this conjunction, and extreme fondness was his inducement to request it.   To be short—he soon died ;   and unhappily for me, not only from sustaining the loss of a valuable and sincere friend, but by the unexpected stroke of death, I was deprived of every hope and means of support.''

Charlotte being in debt, was thrust into the debtors' prison, Marshalsea, but was relieved by a subscription from the coffee-house keepers in Covent Garden. She now adopted masculine attire as her usual wear, and made many conquests among her own sex.   " I appeared as Mr. Brown (a name most hateful to me now, for reasons the town shall have shortly leave to guess at), in a very genteel manner," she relates, " and not making the least discovery of my sex by my behaviour, ever endeavouring to keep up to the well-bred gentleman, I became, as I may most properly term it, the unhappy object of love in a young lady, whose fortune was beyond all earthly power to deprive her of, had it been possible for me to have been what she designed me, nothing less than her husband.   She was an orphan heiress, and under age ;   but so near it, that at the expiration of eight months her guardian resigned his trust, and I might have been at once possessed of the lady and forty thousand pounds in the Bank of England, besides effects in the Indies that were worth about twenty thousand more, which would have been thought an excellent remedy for ills, by those less surrounded with misery than I was.   I, who was the principal player in this tragedy, was the last acquainted with it ;   but

it got wind from the servants to some of the players ;
who as Hamlet says ' can't keep a secret,' and they
immediately communicated it to me.

" Contrary to their expectation, I received the
information with infinite concern ; not more in regard
to myself, than from the poor lady's misfortune, in
placing her affection on an improper object ; and
whom, by letters I afterwards received, confirmed
me, ' she was too fond of her mistaken bargain.'

" The means by which I came by her letters was
through the persuasion of her maid ; who, like most
persons of her function, are too often ready to carry
on intrigues. 'Twas no difficult matter to persuade
an amorous heart to follow its own inclination ; and
accordingly a letter came to invite me to drink tea,
at a place a little distant from the house where she
lived.

" The reason given for this interview was, the
desire some young ladies of her acquaintance had to
hear me sing ; and, as they never went to plays in
the country, 'twould be a great obligation to her if
I would oblige her friends, by complying with her
request.

" The maid who brought this epistle, informed of
the real occasion of its being wrote ; and told me,
if I pleased, I might be the happiest man in the
kingdom, before I was eight-and-forty hours older.
This frank declaration from the servant gave me an
odd opinion of the mistress ; and I sometimes conceived, being conscious how unfit I was to embrace
so favourable an opportunity, that it was all a joke.

" However, be it as it might, I resolved to go and
know the reality. The maid, too, insisted that I
should, and protested her lady had suffered much on
my account, from the first hour she saw me ; and

but for her, the secret had never been disclosed.
She farther added, I was the first person who had ever
made that impression on her mind. I own I felt a
tender concern, and resolved within myself to wait
on her; and by honestly confessing who I was, kill
or cure her hopes of me for ever.

"In obedience to the lady's commands I waited
on her, and found her with two more, much of her
own age, who were her confidantes, and entrusted to
contrive a method to bring this business to an end
by a private marriage. When I went into the room,
I made a general bow to all, but was soon lugged out
of my chair by a young madcap of fashion; and, to
both the lady's confusion and mine, awkwardly
seated by her.

"We were exactly in the condition of Lord Hardy
and Lady Charlotte in *The Funeral*; and I sat with
as much fear in my countenance, as if I had stole
her watch from her side. She, on her part, often
attempted to speak; but had such a tremor on her
voice, she ended only in broken sentences. 'Tis true,
I have undergone the dreadful apprehensions of a
bum-bailiff, but I should have thought one at that
time a seasonable relief, and without repining have
gone with him.

"The before-mentioned madcap, after putting us
more out of countenance by bursting into a violent
fit of laughing, took the other by the sleeve and
withdrew, as she thought to give me a favourable
opportunity of paying my addresses; but she was deceived, for when we were alone, I was in ten thousand
times worse plight than before; and what added to
my confusion, was seeing the poor soul dissolve into
tears, which she endeavoured to conceal.

"This gave me freedom of speech, by a gentle

enquiry into the cause, and by tenderly trying to soothe her into a calm, I unhappily increased, rather than assuaged the dreadful conflict of love and shame which laboured in her bosom.

" With much difficulty I mustered up sufficient courage to open a discourse, by which I began to make a discovery of my name and family, which struck the poor creature into astonishment ; but how much greater was her surprise, when I positively assured her that I was actually the youngest daughter of Mr. Cibber, and not the person she conceived me ! She was absolutely struck speechless for some little time ; but when she regained the power of utterance, entreated me not to urge a falsehood of that nature, which she looked upon only as an evasion, occasioned, she supposed, through a dislike of her person."

In 1755, Charlotte Charke wrote in eight numbers an account of her life, and endeavoured to enlist the sympathies of her father, who had quarrelled with her.

Charlotte Charke to Colley Cibber

" *Saturday, March* 8, 1755.

" HONOURED SIR,

" I doubt not but you are sensible I last Saturday published the first number of a Narrative of my Life, in which I made a proper concession in regard to those unhappy miscarriages which have for many years justly deprived me of a father's fondness. As I am conscious of my errors, I thought I could not be too public in sueing for your blessing and pardon ; and only blush to think, my youthful follies should draw so strong a compunction on my mind in the meridian of my days, which I might have so easily avoided.

" Be assured, Sir, I am perfectly convinced I was more than much to blame ; and that the hours of anguish I have felt have bitterly repaid me for the commission of every indiscretion, which was the un-happy motive of being so many years estranged from that happiness I now, as in duty-bound, most earnestly implore.

" I shall, with your permission, Sir, send again, to know if I may be admitted to throw myself at your feet ; and, with sincere and filial transport, en-deavour to convince you that I am,

" Honoured Sir,

" Your truly penitent and dutiful daughter,

" CHARLOTTE CHARKE."

Cibber, however, was so incensed with his daughter that he returned the letter, by the messenger who brought it, in a blank envelope.

To support herself and her daughter, Charlotte Charke did many strange things. For some time, she subsisted as a higgler, with, she says, tolerable success. She acted as a valet-de-chambre to a noble-man—who never suspected her sex. She performed at the booths at New Wells, during Bartholomew Fair, where her remuneration must have been incon-siderable. She was for a short time a waiter at a coffee-house, run by a Mrs. Dorr. Whatever else she had, she had courage. " In regard to my child," she relates :

" I begged not to be obliged to lie in the house, but constantly came to my time in a morning, and stayed till about ten or eleven at night ; and have often wondered I have escaped without wounds or blows from the gentlemen of the paf, who are numerous and frequent in their evening patrols through these

An exact Representation of Mr Charke walking in the Ditch at four Years of Age, as described by herself in the first Number of the Narrative of her own Life, lately published.

London Published According to Act of Parliament Sepr 6th 1755.

CHARLOTTE CHARKE
After F. Garden

fields, and my march extended as far as Long Acre, by which means I was obliged to pass through the thickest of 'em. But Heaven everlastingly be praised! I never had any encounter with 'em, and used to jog along with the air of a raw, unthinking, penniless apprentice, which I suppose rendered me not worthy their observation.

" In the week-days, business (though good) was not so very brisk as on Sundays, so that when I had any leisure hours I employed them in working in the garden, which I was then capable of doing with some small judgment; but that and everything else created fresh surprise in my mistress, who behaved to me as if I had been rather her son than her servant."

Charlotte returned to the Haymarket, then under the management of her brother, and, later, went on a tour of the provincial theatres. She turned her hand to many a thing, but always without success. She even conceived the idea of becoming a hog merchant.

" As I found one business fall off," she writes, " I resolved to set up another, and went in one of my extraordinary hurries to buy a sow with pig; but, to my great disappointment, after having kept it for near three months, expecting it hourly to bring forth, it proved to be an old barrow : and I, to make up the measure of my prudent management, after having put myself to double the expense it cost me in the purchase, was glad to sell it to a butcher for a shilling or two less than I gave for it.

" Thus ended my notion of being a hog merchant, and I having a garden well stored with fruits of all sorts, made the best I could of that, till some villainous wretches, in one night's time, robbed me of as much as would have yielded near three guineas, besides barbarously tearing up the trees by the roots, and

K

breaking the branches through fearful haste ; being well assured that the gentleman who owned them would have punished them to the utmost rigour of the law, had they been discovered."

Besides *The Art of Management*, Charlotte wrote two other plays, *The Carnival, or, Harlequin Blunderer*, which was acted at the theatre in Lincoln's Inn Fields in 1735 ; and *Tit for Tat, or, Comedy and Tragedy at War*, performed at Punch's Theatre in St. James's Street, in 1743. Further she was responsible for two novels, *The Lover's Treat, or, Unnatural Hatred*, and *The History of Henry Dumont, Esq., and Miss Charlotte Evelyn, with some Critical Remarks on Comic Actors*.

Let unfortunate and unhappy Charlotte Charke sum up her own life :—

" This day, April 19, 1755, is published, the eighth and last number of a Narrative of the Life of Mrs. Charlotte Charke, with a dedication from and to myself : the properest patron I could have chosen, as I am most likely to be tenderly partial to my poetical errors, and will be as bounteous in the reward, as we may reasonably imagine my merit can claim.

" This work, contains, first,—A notable promise of entertaining the town with the history of Henry Dumont, Esq., and Miss Charlotte Evelyn ; but, being universally known to be an odd product of nature, was requested to postpone that, and give an account of myself, from my infancy to the present time.

" Secondly,—My natural propensity to a hat and wig, in which at the age of four years, I made a very considerable figure in a ditch, with several other succeeding pranks. An account of my education at

Westminster. Why did not I make a better use of so happy an advantage!

"Thirdly,—My extraordinary skill in the science of physic, with a recommendation of the necessary use of snails and gooseberry leaves, when drugs and chemical preparations were not comeatable. My natural aversion to a needle, and profound respect for a currycomb, in the use of which I excelled most young ladies in Great Britain. My extensive knowledge in gardening; not forgetting that necessary accomplishment for a young gentlewoman, in judiciously discharging a blunderbuss or a fowling piece. My own, and the lucky escape of life, when I ran over a child at Uxbridge.

"Fourthly,—My indiscreetly plumping into the sea of matrimony, and becoming a wife before I had the proper understanding of a reasonable child. An account of my coming on the stage. My uncommon success there. My folly in leaving it. My recommendation of my sister Marples to the consideration of every person who chooses to eat an elegant meal, or chat away a few moments with a humorous, good-natured elderly landlady. My turning grocer, with some wise remarks on the rise and fall of sugars and teas. An unfortunate adventure in selling a link. A short account of my father and mother's courtship and marriage.

"Fifthly,—A faithful promise to prefer a bill in Chancery against my uncle's widow, who has artfully deprived his heirs at law of a very considerable fortune.—N.B. The old dame may be assured I will be as good as my word.—My keeping a grand puppet-show, and losing as much money by it as it cost me. My becoming a widow, and being afterwards privately married; which, as it proved, I had better have let alone. My going into men's clothes, in which I continued many years, the reason of which I beg to be excused, as it concerns no mortal now living but myself. My becoming a second time a widow, which drew on me inexpressible sorrows, that lasted upwards of twelve years, and the unforeseen turns of providence, by which I was constantly extricated from them. An unfortunate interview with a fair lady, who would have made me master of herself and fortune, if I had been lucky enough to have been in reality what I appeared.

" Sixthly,—My endeavouring at a reconciliation with my father. His sending back my letter in a blank. His being too much governed by humour, but more so by her, whom age cannot exempt from being the lively limner of her own face; which she had better neglect a little, and pay part of that regard to what she ought to esteem the nobler part, and must have an existence when her painted frame is reduced to ashes.

" Seventhly,—My being gentleman to certain peer; after my dismission, becoming an occasional player, while I was playing bo-peep with the world. My turning pork merchant; broke, through the inhuman appetite of a hungry dog. Went a strolling. Several adventures during my peregrination. My return, and setting up an eating house in Drury Lane; undone again, by pilfering lodgers. Turning drawer at St. Marylabonne. Going to the Haymarket theatre with my brother. His leaving it. Many distresses arising on that account. Going strolling a second time, and staying near nine years. Several remarkable occurrences while I was abroad; particularly my being sent to G—— gaol, for being an actor; which, to do most strolling players justice, they ought not to have the laws enforced against them on that score, for a very substantial reason. My settling in Wales, and turning pastrycook and farmer. Made a small mistake in turning hog merchant. Went to the seat of destruction called Pill : broke, and came away. Hired myself to a printer at Bristol, to write, and correct the press. Made a short stay there. Vagabondised again, and last Christmas returned to London, where I hope to remain as long as I live."

Charlotte Charke's last days were spent in abject poverty. Samuel Whyte, in a communication to the *Monthly Magazine*, has given a description of her surroundings : " Her habitation was a wretched thatched hovel, situate on the way to Islington, not very distant from the New River Head, where it was usual at that time for the scavengers to deposit the sweepings of the street. The night preceding, a heavy rain had fallen, which rendered this extraordinary seat of the muses nearly inaccessible and we could only approach by wading almost knee-deep in mud. We did not attempt to pull the latch-string, but knocked at the door, which was opened by a tall, meagre, ragged figure, with a blue apron, indicating, what otherwise was doubtful, that it was a female before us ; a perfect model for the Copper Captain's tattered landlady, that deplorable exhibition of the fair sex in the comedy of *Rule a Wife and Have a Wife*. With a torpid voice and constrained smile, she desired us to walk in. The first object that presented itself was a dresser—clean, it must be confessed, but wretchedly furnished ; to the right sat the mistress of the house, on a broken chair under the mantel-piece, by a fire merely sufficient to put us in mind of starving. At our author's feet, on the flounce of her dingy petticoat, reclined a dog, almost a skeleton, who saluted us with a snarl. 'Have done, Fidele! these are friends.' The tone of her voice had something in it humbled and disconsolate, a mingled effort of authority and pleasure. Poor soul! few were her visitors of that description; no wonder the creature barked. A magpie was perched on the top rail of her chair, and on her lap was placed a pair of mutilated bellows—the pipe was gone. These were used as a substitute for a writing-desk, on which lay displayed her hopes and treasure, the manuscript of her novel. A rough deal-board, with three hobbling supporters, was brought for our convenience; on which, without farther ceremony, we contrived to sit down, and enter into business. The work was read, remarks made, alterations suggested and agreed to, and thirty guineas demanded for the copy. The squalid handmaid, who had been attentive listener, stretched forth her tawny neck with an eye of anxious expectation. The bookseller offered five guineas. Our authoress did not appear hurt; disappointment had rendered her mind callous: however, some altercation ensued, and was terminated by the bookseller doubling his first proposal, which was accepted."

Charlotte Charke shall here give her apologia : " I cannot recollect any crime I have been guilty of that is unpardonable, which the denial of my request may possibly make the world believe I have ; but I dare challenge the most malicious tongue of slander to a proof of that kind, as heaven and my own conscience can equally acquit me of having deserved that dreadful sentence of not being forgiven."

MARGARET (" PEG ") WOFFINGTON
1714 ?–1760

MARGARET ("PEG") WOFFINGTON
1714 ?–1760

INCOMPARABLE Peg ! She made havoc of all hearts—save those of her theatrical rivals. Indeed, to know her was to love her—and she was not indisposed to be loved. The tale of her admirers is long—and to many of them she was kind. When she was playing the " breeches part " of Sir Harry Wildair in Farquhar's *The Constant Couple,* she said proudly to Quin, she believed that half the audience thought her to be a man, to which the embittered old gentleman replied, " Perhaps, but the other half *knows* you are a woman." These two sparred frequently, though in all amity. When Quin once asked why she had been to Bath when she should have been at Covent Garden, she answered with her usual sauciness, " Oh, for mere wantonness." Whereupon he retorted, " And have you been cured ? "

Margaret Woffington—to give her correct name, though no one called her other than " Peg "—was born in Dublin. The year of her birth is in dispute. Fitzgerald Molloy gives it as about 1719, and another writer as October 1718 ; but Joseph Knight thinks it was probably 1714. Her father was a working bricklayer, who died in 1720, and had a pauper's funeral. He left a widow, who, to support herself and her two children, Peg and Mary, kept a huckster's shop on Ormonde Quay ; but, failing, was reduced to hawking fruit and vegetables in the streets. One day, Madame Violante, a Frenchwoman, was giving a miscellaneous entertainment in a booth, saw Peg, was attracted by her looks, and offered to engage her. Fitzgerald Molloy has conjured up the scene in his own imaginative manner :

" At the close of an October day, in the year 1727, a child of about eight years old slowly tottered along Ormond Quay, Dublin, under the weight of a pitcher of water which she carried on her head. The evening had set dark and cold, and promised a bleak and dreary night. Already the sky was overcast with heavy clouds, a sad voiced north-east wind sweeping up the sluggish Liffey, carried with it a chill pene-trating mist that gradually increased to drenching rain. Heavily framed lamps, imprisoning the poor wan light of oil wicks, swung with many a creak from the corner houses of dreary streets and black-looking alleys, or hung above the old stone bridges with quaint and ponderous balustrades, and but-tresses green and slimy from the ebb and flow of countless tides, casting a patch of light upon the black waters beneath, as if seeking crimes and mysteries hidden in their depths. A few passengers, with heads bowed low, and cloaks and coats drawn tightly round them to avoid the bitter wind, hastened to and fro, shadow-like in the deepening gloom. A coach or two rattled with noisy haste, over the uneven pave-ments. The bells of the church clocks rang out six, their sounds falling faint and changeful, like fright-ened voices crying for help from the heights of steeples and towers, upon which the vapour and cloud had already descended.

" With the wind blowing in her face, the rain dashing on her scarcely covered limbs, the child, labouring under the weight of her pitcher, made but slow way. At last, shivering in her wet rags, and overcome by her misery, she burst into tears ; raised her arms above her head, removed the pitcher, and sought the passing shelter of an open doorway. She had scarcely wiped the rain from her face with the remains of an old tattered and colourless shawl which helped to cover her shoulders, when a lady, who had for some time followed her, also sought protection in the hall, faintly lit by the flickering rays of a lamp.

" ' You are cold, my childe,' said the lady, looking at her keenly.

" ' Yes, ma'am,' said the girl, raising her eyes, expressive of surprise to the stranger's face.

" Even in her rags the child looked picturesque. Her dark, unkempt hair curled naturally round a well-shaped head, and hung above a wide, low forehead ; her eyes, large and liquid, seemed almost black under the shadow of their long lashes, and the full sweeping curve of her brows ; her cheeks were pale and beautifully oval ; her lips somewhat full and red : whilet her prettily dimpled chin gave a piquant look to the lower part of her face, which the sweet gravity of her eyes contradicted.

" ' And what is your name, my leetle childe ? ' said the lady in a voice to which a foreign accent gave a peculiar softness.

" ' Me name is Peg, ma'am,' said the girl, opening wide her eyes, made all the brighter by the tears which yet glistened in them.

" ' Peg, it is a pretty name. But is there no other ? ' asked the lady, pushing back the dark, tangled locks with a touch that was caressing in its gentleness.

" ' Peg Woffington, ma'am,' said the girl, pleased with the lady's attentions,

" ' And where you live, eh, leetle Peg Woffington ?
Is it far from here, eh ? ' continued the foreign lady,
letting her eyes wander from the child's handsome
face to her limbs, rounded and shaped with wonderful
grace.

" ' Not far, ma'am,' said Peg. ' Me mother lives
in George's Court. She is a widee ; an' she washes
for the neighbours ' ; and so saying she cast her eyes
on the pitcher of water by her side, as if some train of
thought had suddenly suggested itself to her mind.
' An' this is washing day ; an' I've been carryin' jugs
o' water since dinner. But this is the last of 'em ; an'
—an' I must go now, ma'am ; for there's no sign o'
the rain stoppin' an' mother will be wonderin' what
keeps me,' said Peg, stooping to raise her burden on
her head once more.

" ' And I shall go with you,' said the lady, with
that foreign accent which gave her voice so sweet a
sound.

" The child set the pitcher down again, straight-
ened herself, and looked at the lady with eyes expressive of wonder.

" ' I am,' said the lady, ' Madame Violante. You
perhaps have heard my name ? '

" ' What ! ' said Peg, in greater amazement now
than ever ; for at the mention of that name there
rose before her the vision of a great booth in Fownes
Court, with a vast glare of lights, where the sounds of
fiddles and drums were heard strumming and beating
right merry measures, and to which crowds flocked
nightly, that they might see such tricks and daring
feats as had never before been witnessed in this goodly
city.

" ' And you are Madame' Lante, that dances on
the rope ? ' said Peg, looking down at the lady's feet,

as if by her glance she would unravel the mystery by which the celebrated dancer nightly balanced herself on a tight-rope and skipped upon a slackwire above the heads of applauding crowds.

"'The same,' said the French lady, smiling. 'Would you like to dance also on the rope—— '

"'And wear such beautiful dresses, with spangles ? ' interrupted this juvenile daughter of Eve. 'Oh, ma'am, I would be delighted ! '

"'Very well, I will teach you,' said Violante.

"'And I shall wear a star on me forehead, ma'am, when I dance—like you ? ' she asked.

"'Yes,' answered Madame Violante, 'if you learn quickly and well. But first we must ask your mother, and hear what she will say ; show me the way to her house, and whilst we go you can tell me all about yourself, my childe.'

"So Peg lifted the earthenware pitcher, that seemed now no heavier than a feather, and placed it on her shapely head, and went out into the darkness which was almost as of night. Her steps were so light and quick that her new friend could scarcely keep pace with her ; the rain and the wind were unheeded, though the one pattered on her face, and the other sent the poor rags fluttering from her rounded limbs. Presently they left the exposed quays and turned up a dark narrow street, with high, black-looking houses on either side, in the friendly shelter of which the child in answer to the Frenchwoman's questions told her that she and her mother and her little sister were as poor as church mice, since, said she, 'the doctors, the devil take 'em, killed me father when he had the faver a few years ago ; an' sure 'twas the first time in his life he ever had 'em to attend him, and 'twas his last. God be good to his sowl ; but they say the doctors are never lucky, and they kill a mighty lot o' people anyhow. An' me mother,' she continued, ' takes in washin', an' works hard all day, an' at night she sells oranges outside the door o' the playhouse in Aungier Street ; an' never a much she makes be that same ; an' as for meself, sometimes I sell oranges too, an' sallad for a ha'penny a dish, an' water cresses in the sayson ; and the young gentlemen in Trinity College behave decent to me, an' often give me a penny for nothin' at all, only because I talk to them, an' make them laugh ; an' they're not bad, poor fellows anyhow, when they have the money ; but sure there are times when they're just as poor as meself a'most, an' it's many a time I popped their clothes for them, comin' to the end o' the month, you know. But they're rale good hearted, an' they like me well.'

" At the end of this dark street they turned into a lane on the right, and finally entered an unsavoury court, lighted only by dim rays of tallow candles shining through the small paned windows of the surrounding hovels. Quickly gliding into one of them, the child mounted a rickety stair, loudly calling out to her mother that a lady was coming to see her. At this information, a woman wearing a deep bordered blowsy cap that had once been white, and a cotton gown, the sleeves of which were rolled to the shoulders, displaying her red and smoking arms fresh from the wash tub, hastily took a candle from a tin sconce nailed to the whitewashed wall, and rushing forward with it, held it above the creaking stairway in a position most favourable to the descent of melted tallow on her visitor's head.

" ' Walk in, ma'am, an' welcome,' said the hostess, foreseeing in her mind's eye an additional customer

to the wash tub.   Restoring the candle to the sconce,
she made a rush at the best chair the poor room con-
tained, and rubbed it heartily with her apron, which
she afterwards applied in the same manner to her
perspiring face.

"'An' won't you sit down, ma'am?' she continued,
peering into the stranger's countenance through an
atmosphere which was rendered a trifle misty by
smoke from the turf fire, and steam from the wash
tub.   ' Peg, stir the cradle and don't let Polly wake.
Do you hear me ? '

"'Mother,' said Peg, feeling herself called on to
make some introduction, ' it's Madame 'Lante,' add-
ing, after a moment's pause, ' the lady that dances
on the rope.'   And so saying, the child made a curtsey,
not without grace, to her visitor.

" Being favoured with this introduction the dan-
seuse seated herself, and explained the motive of her
visit. She had been struck by the beauty of Peg's face,
and by the grace and bearing of her figure, and
offered to take her as an apprentice and teach her
the business of a tight-rope dancer. The poor washer-
woman dried her arms, opened her eyes very wide,
and looked bewildered at the unexpected proposal
which was so suddenly laid before her.

"' It will be well for the leetle Peg ; she will earn
good salaries in a short times,' put in Madame Violante, ' and I will dress and support her.'

" At this prospect a shrewd twinkle came into
Mrs. Woffington's eyes. She knew the value of money.

"' Well, ma'am,' she said, putting her arms akimbo,
' none of me blood has ever been playactors or ever
danced upon a rope ; an' for the matter o' that me
mother's people never disgraced themselves be earn-
ing a penny piece, but lived upon their 'states like

the highest in the land ; an' sure, 'twas often tould
us the head of the family was one o' the rale kings of
Ireland himself. But sure, that was in the good owld
times, and there's no use in talking o' them, and here
am I, only a poor widee-woman, God help me, with
two children to support, an' the times mighty hard,
and me good man took from me with little or no
warning, God help us ! An' it's a miserable world we
live in.'

" ' It was sad,' the sympathetic Frenchwoman said,
taking advantage of a slight pause in the widow's
autobiographical sketch.

" ' An' sure, everyone knows, ma'am,' she continued, ' that you bear the character of an honest
woman, an' not like most o' them wenches belonging
to the playhouse. An' sure as you say Peggy might
earn a dacent livin' in a little while, an' that you will
support and clothe the child, sure you may take her,
an' I'll pray God to protect her,' said the washer-
woman."

One of the items in the performance was that
Madame Violante crossed the stage on a tight-rope,
with a basket on each foot containing a baby. Peg
was one of the babies. It must have been an anxious
time for Peg's mother. The " miscellaneous entertainment " failed to attract, and was closed down.
Peg then assisted her parent to the best of her power.
Better things, however, were in store for her.
Madame Violante did not lose sight of her, and,
when she was ten, again engaged her for a children's
company which was starting. So began the great
actress's career. She played Polly Peachum in *The
Beggar's Opera* to the Macheath of Betty Barnes
(afterwards Mrs. Workman), Nell in *The Devil to Pay*,
and other parts. Not only did Peg thus early acquire

MARGARET WOFFINGTON
Artist unknown

a sense of the theatre, but was trained by Madame Violante, who had taken a great liking to her, in deportment and elocution, and, busy woman as she was, taught her French. This was all the education she received : whatever else she came to know she acquired for herself.

Thomas Elrington, a well-known London actor, acquired, on the death of his father-in-law, Joseph Ashbury, in 1720, the management of the Smock Alley Theatre in Dublin, and made a great success of it, both financial and artistic. He saw Peg ; was delighted by her performances, and gave her an engagement. At what date this was cannot be said, but it must have been before she was eighteen—some years before, probably—because Elrington died in 1732. She often had to dance between the acts, and was occasionally given elderly parts, such as Mrs. Peachum in *The Beggar's Opera* and Mother Midnight in Farquhar's *The Twin Rivals*—excellent training for a novice. Peg never hesitated to sacrifice her appearance to her art. " In Mrs. Day in *The Committee*," Davies says in his biography of David Garrick, " Mrs. Woffington made no scruple to disguise her beautiful countenance, by drawing on it the lines of deformity and the wrinkles of old age, and to put on the tawdry habiliments and vulgar manners of an old hypocritical city vixen." Even in 1749, when she could choose her part, or at least reject any that did not appeal to her, she was content to create Veturia in Thomson's *Coriolanus*, though she had to paint wrinkles on her lovely face. Peg was in constant employ for some years either at Smock Alley Theatre ; or with Sparks and Barrington, at the theatre in Rainsford Street. To pass over this period quickly—she played Ophelia in April 1737 at the Smock Alley Theatre ; where

L

she repeated her performance of Polly Peachum. In April 1740 she made her first great hit in " breeches part "—Sir Harry Wildair.

" About this time an event happened which may be considered the turning-point in her career : she fell in love," so runs another of Fitzgerald Molloy's fanciful pictures. " The object of her affection was a young gentleman of position but of small fortune, named Taaffe, the third son of a needy Irish peer. He was not only delighted with her talents as an actress, but fascinated by her beauty as a woman. He was a man well to look upon, tall and of goodly shape ; with sea-blue eyes, light brown hair, and a smile as bright, if, alas, as deceptive as April sunshine. Night after night he sat in the boxes of the theatre, watching the play of her face that was more beautiful than health ; the glamour of her lustrous eyes ; the smiles that played round a mouth like unto a cleft pomegranate ; the turn of the head ; the movement of the graceful limbs. When she left the stage, he felt as if sudden darkness had descended upon him. She was to him what sunlight is to the world. By day he wooed her with soft words and gentle looks, and many endearments, with all the passion, the longing, and the pain of his youth ; for he thought no woman ever was born so beautiful as she. And, as a woman, she loved him, not wisely, but too well ; trusting him with the precious treasure of her honour, resting confident that because of her vast affection for him, he would in return make her his lawful wife. At his request she quitted the stage at a time when the promise of a great career shone before her ; at his desire she left her native city to accompany him to London. For she loved him all in all." The lovers came to London, and lived to-

gether in York Street, Covent Garden. Of course,
the affair could not go on indefinitely. Taaffe was
away from her more and more; and one day told
her he must go back for a few weeks to Ireland to
attend to some business. As a matter of fact, his
affairs were in a bad way; but he proposed to remedy
that, not by going to Ireland, but by paying his
addresses to a considerable heiress, Miss Dallaway,
who naturally was ignorant of his connection with
Peg Woffington. In due course, the news was conveyed to the young actress, who was overcome
with fury at the duplicity of her lover, and
determined to avenge herself. This was easier
thought than done. At last, an idea occurred to her.
She remembered her success as Sir Harry Wildair,
and decided to make the acquaintance of Miss Dallaway in the attire of a young man of fashion. She
soon contrived to find someone to introduce her at
Vauxhall. The rest of the story is dramatic—the
whole of it is perhaps apocryphal—but as Molloy
has printed it, it shall be told here in his own
words.

" ' I believe, sir, by your conversation, that you
live in town,' said the lady, laying her hand on his
arm as lightly as might be.

" ' At present, yes, madam,' says he, ' I have,
however, been here but a few short months, having
arrived in the spring from—from one of the univer-
sities.'

" ' Young gentlemen are taught many things there,'
says she.

" ' Yes, madam,' replies he with a wicked smile,
' in the one from which I came they learned many
things—from me.'

" ' From you, sir ! ' stealing a glance at him.

" ' That is, I taught them some very pretty manners—I have always been famed for my manners.'

" ' Of that I have no doubt, sir,' replied the lady.

" ' But alas, madam,' the gentleman said with a
sigh, ' I find that I have come to town too late.'

" He felt as if he were playing a part ; the habit
of acting, difficult to lay aside even in serious
moments, was now strong upon him ; the gardens
with their lights and music were but a stage ; the
surroundings but theatrical accessories ; and the
purport for which he had donned this disguise, and
sallied forth upon the town for the last week, but a
plot of a comedy. And yet it was all real, terribly
real, and under the bravery of that broidered waistcoat beat a woman's heart that was sick from grief,
yet strong for revenge.

" ' Too late ? May I venture to inquire why you
say so ? ' said Miss Dallaway.

" ' If I only dared to tell her,' said the gentleman,
in that undertone called on the stage an aside, which,
though quite audible, is supposed to be unheard.
Then he added in a louder tone, ' Too late, madam,
to secure my own happiness.'

" ' How do you mean ? ' queried Miss Dallaway,
who seemed to conceive a sudden interest in the cause
of his distress.

" ' When I came to town,' said he, lifting his eyes
to hers, and catching a look of pleasure which promised a deeper concern in his affairs, ' I heard the
name of Miss Dallaway on every tongue. In the
coffee-houses it was spoken with respectful admiration, in all polite assemblies with unmeasured praise.
Everywhere her beauties and qualities were vastly
lauded, until I grew impatient to see the object of
such general esteem. But when at last good fortune

permitted me to see her—when I saw you, madam, I knew that all I had heard had not done justice to your perfections ; I saw that your merits were as far superior to the compliments which every tongue had uttered, as glorious day is to the darkness of night, as heaven itself is to this poor earth.'

" ' Oh ! sir,' said the lady, blushing, ' you over-whelm me.'

" ' Nay, Madam,' said the gallant, ' I speak but the naked truth.   But with the knowledge of your per-fections, came also the news that you had given your love, your life, to the keeping of one who had been happy enough to find favour in your eyes.'

" ' That is true, Sir,' said the lady, as if the fact had been suddenly recalled to her, and recalled with-out pleasure ; ' he—he is a gentleman of worth,' she added.

" ' If he were indeed one likely to render you happy, madam,' said the gallant, ' I would never have sought this interview to-night.'

" ' What do you mean, sir ? ' said Miss Dallaway, with a change of tone that indicated both surprise and displeasure.

" ' I mean,' he answered boldly, ' that he is un-worthy of your esteem and love ; that in fact, Madam, he is a worthless fellow and a profligate.'

" ' It is false,' she said, indignantly removing her hand from her companion's arm.   ' This is a charge trumped up to blacken his character in my eyes, an unworthy trick to ingratiate yourself in my favour ; but, clever as you are, Sir, it shall not succeed.'

" ' Upon my honour, Madam, it is true,' said Mr. Adair very quietly ' I see you love him too, and I grieve to pain you—in truth I do ; but this gentle-man is well known, as I have recently learned, for his gallantries. Nay, bear with me whilst I tell you, that even while he made love to you from mercenary motives, he was carrying on an affair with an actress whom he brought to town from Ireland.'

"'An actress?' she gasped, pale now, and trembling all over. Then, the colour coming back into her cheeks, she cried out, 'I'll not believe it; it cannot be possible that the man who swore he loved me—loved me better than all the world besides, loved me for myself alone—is false to me. Take back your words; say, they are untrue, the trick of a rival in a war of love—or' (with a change of tone no longer pleading, but commanding) 'produce one proof that your words are true.'

"'Madam,' said the Woffington, for it was no longer the man of fashion, but the woman who now spoke, 'I cannot take back my words; but, as it may be well for you to know this man, I will show you proof that what I have said is true.' And she drew out a bundle of letters, some of them of recent date, some of them well worn because often read. 'You know the writing?'

"The young lady fixed her eyes on them for a second, and nodded her head.

"'Then read them,' said the Woffington.

"In her haste, Miss Dallaway almost tore the squarely folded sheets of paper bearing Taaffe's seal, and his characters to Mrs. Margaret Woffington, and read line after line that spoke of love and faithfulness for this actress, until the letters seemed to burn themselves into her brain; then the music of the band fell fainter and fainter on her ears, her head swam, and, with a low cry, she tottered forward, and would have fallen, but that Peg Woffington caught her in her outstretched arms. The place was quite solitary; no one had witnessed this scene. With an effort Peg Woffington lifted the insensible girl to a bench close by, fanned her face, and chafed her hands.

"'Poor girl,' she said, 'I did not think she loved him so! What fools we women are!' Tears sprang into her eyes, and bending down her head, she kissed the girl's forehead with tenderness. 'Did you know me, you would shrink from the touch of my lips,' she said, almost in a whisper, and again she kissed her with the love of a sister.

"In a little while the young lady opened her eyes, and looking round her, remembered all.

"'My child,' said the Woffington, tenderly forgetting completely the character she assumed, 'I have caused you some pain, but from suffering, good often springs. It is best that you should know the man to whom you were about to trust the happiness of your whole life as he really is. When next a man pleads to you, have more care regarding his character, before you give him the treasure of your love.'

"'You have saved me,' said the girl. 'I loved him, and now—now—— '

"'You see he is unworthy of you. My task has been, after all, an ungracious one; and when I undertook it I had no thought for the trouble it might bring you. Forgive me.'

"'Then it was not to save me you told me this?' said Miss Dallaway wonderingly.

"'No; it was to punish him for his deception to —to one very near to me,' said the Woffington; her cheeks were burning.

"'In any case, I owe you thanks,' said the young lady, while tears almost choked her voice. 'Your words are kind; surely, ah! surely your heart must be good.'

" ' Good ? If you knew me you would not say so,'
said the Woffington. Then she hesitated just for a
second ; longing, in obedience to some sudden impulse, to throw off the character she had assumed,
and reveal herself ; yet fearing to lose the regard
which she had gained, and dreading the dislike and
distrust which she knew her name must call up.
Suddenly resuming her former air of a coxcomb, she
therefore laughed airily and said, ' Madam, believe
me I am no better than my neighbours.'

" Miss Dallaway rose up, puzzled by the contra-
dictions in manner and tone which this young man's
manner betrayed.

" ' Let us seek my friends,' she said. ' I'm sure
they have missed me.'

" She held out her hand, which the Woffington took
in both of hers and raised it to her lips not with affected
gallantry, but in honest pity. Then arm in arm, and
without exchanging another word they went forth
amongst the crowd.

" The first light of a summer day had crept into
the sky before the Woffington reached her lodgings
in York Street, Covent Garden. In obedience to the
loud summons of one of her chairmen, the door was
quickly opened, not by a servant, but by her lover,
who had just returned. She started for a moment
in surprise ; then, getting out of the chair, she quickly
passed him, and entered the house, leaving him to
wrangle with the chairmen. Passing into the sitting-
room, she flung off her dainty gold-laced hat and
powdered wig, loosened her cravat, undid her sword,
cast it from her on the floor impatiently, and then
sat down in a great chair to await his coming. Her
mood had changed. The manner of a man about
town had vanished completely ; the air of reckless

audacity had given place to the weariness of re-
action; the scene in which she had so cleverly
enacted a part, now affected her in an unlooked-
for degree, and filled her with bitter self-reproach.

" ' Well, Peggy,' said Taaffe, entering the room with
a blithe air, ' have you no word of welcome for me
after coming back to you four days sooner than I
expected.'

" ' I am tired,' she answered, shortly, without
looking at him.

" Her face was white and haggard seen by this
early light; there was a dangerous glitter in her dark
eyes, a defiant air in her bearing.

" ' Ah, I see,' said he with a short laugh. ' You
have been out amusing yourself at your old stage
tricks again, and donning the breeches.'

" Coming over to where she was, he sat down beside
her, and stretched out his arms as if to caress her,
with such tenderness as was his wont in the first
days of their courtship. The same light was in his
sea-blue eyes, the same smile on his lips which had
first dazzled her, filled her heart with a torrent of
happiness, and made her weigh the world light in the
balance of his love. But now she saw only the weakness, the deception, and cruelty of his nature reflected
in his eyes and playing on his lips, and she shrank
from him.

" ' Don't touch me,' she said, in a tone such as he
had never heard her use before. He did not dare to
disobey her.

" ' Why,' said he, ' it's in a mighty bad temper you
are; you don't seem to have got much diversion out
of your night.'

" ' I have got none,' she answered him, briefly.

" ' It's sorry I am for it,' he said conciliatingly. ' And may I ask where you have been ? '

" ' You may, for I intend telling you. Though I may act many parts, I cannot play the hypocrite like you.' This time she looked him in the face.

" ' What the devil do you mean by that civil speech ? ' asked the gentleman, beginning to comprehend her humour.

" ' I mean,' she answered, ' that I have seen Miss Dallaway, the woman you promised to marry, and I have told her all.'

" ' Good God ! ' cried he, nervously, grasping hold of his chair. ' Is this a part of your play-acting, or is it true ? Answer me at once—— '

" ' It is true,' she replied, unflinchingly meeting the look of horror that crept into his face.

" ' You are a devil ! ' he almost hissed between his clenched teeth.

" ' I am a woman,' she said, rising to her feet, and throwing back her finely turned head with so sudden a gesture, that her long black hair fell in a lustrous shower upon her shoulders—' I am a woman, and you have deceived me. I loved you with all my heart, and you played me false. You swore fidelity to me, and then left me to whisper the same words in the ear of another dupe of your flattering speeches and soft ways. All the love I once bore you turned to hate, and I determined to expose you as the liar and hypocrite that you are.'

" Her eyes flashed, her breasts heaved with passion, her face flushed with the crimson of indignation. She was beautiful ; but the man before her thought only of the injury she had done him. His anger blinded him to the loveliness that once had fascinated him, and he rose up and cursed her.

" ' Tell me what you have done,' he gasped, seeing it was better for him to know the worst at once. ' What have you said to her.'

" ' I have told her that you are a profligate,' she said, looking at him steadily. ' I have told her that even whilst you spoke words of love to her, you were carrying on an affair with—with an actress you had brought with you from Ireland.'

" The words came as if wrenched from her.

" ' She will not believe you,' he said, clutching at some straw by which he might yet be saved.

" ' I have taken care that she shall. I have shown her your letters to me,' she answered.

" ' Good God ! I am undone,' he cried out in despair. ' Do you know that you have ruined me ? My affairs are going to the devil. She is an heiress ; I was to have married her in a couple of weeks, and her fortune would have saved me. You have destroyed me.'

" Woman-like, she began to relent. He strode up and down the room with uneven steps ; his face pale as death, his brows knitted in anger, his lips twitching from the passion of his despair.

" ' I only know,' she answered back, with strongly imposed calmness, ' that you have deceived me. It was enough for me.'

" ' You—you are a tigress,' he replied, hoarse with rage ; and snatching up his cloak and hat, he rushed out of the room and out of the house without another word, nay, even without looking back at her."

Peg Woffington now decided to return to the stage. The Dublin theatres were, of course, open to her ; but she now decided to go out for the bigger game, and to appear in London. An account of her first inter- view with Rich, the manager of Covent Garden

Theatre has been given in the *Memoirs of the Celebrated Mrs. Woffington*. " To the residence of John Rich, situated in the then highly fashionable quarter of Bloomsbury Square, Peg Woffington betook herself, and demanded an interview with the eccentric manager ; but as she refused to give her name, she found this no easy matter to obtain. According to John Galt, she paid no less than nineteen visits before she was admitted. At last she told the servant to say Miss Woffington desired to speak to Mr. Rich, when the man returned with apologies, and, informing her his master would see her at once, showed her in to his private apartment. Entering the room, she found the manager lounging on a sofa, a book in one hand, a china cup, from which he occasionally sipped tea, in another, whilst around him were seven-and-twenty cats, engaged in the various occupations of staring at him, licking his tea-cup, eating the toast from his mouth, walking round his shoulders, and frisking about him with the freedom of long-standing pets."

Why Peg did not send in her name at once, it is not easy to guess, for her reputation had preceded her from Dublin, and she would unquestionably have been received at once. As it was, Rich at once engaged her for Covent Garden at a salary of nine pounds a week.

Quin lost no time in " trying out " his new acquisition. The Irish actress made her first appearance in London on November 6, 1740, as Silvia in *The Recruiting Officer*, in which character she had to masquerade as a boy. Playing with her were Ryan as Plume, and Colley Cibber as Brazen. She at once became a London " star." Her next two parts were Lady Sadlife in *The Double Gallant*, and Aura in Charles Johnston's *The Country Lasses*. Then, on

November 21, she appeared as Sir Harry Wildair—
and the Town was at her feet. The play was performed for ten nights consecutively—then an unusual
thing—and ten times more during the season. Knight
says, " she was so successful in the part that no male
actor was thenceforth acceptable in it."

Next year, presumably having quarrelled with
Rich, Peg accepted an engagement at Drury Lane,
where she was equally successful. Having, then,
established herself as a favourite in London, she returned in the summer of 1742 to Dublin, where, of
course, the reputation she had made was well known,
and added to her popularity.

Peg Woffington had at Drury Lane played Cordelia
to the King Lear of David Garrick. When these two
first met is not known. It had been said that it was
soon after Peg came to London, when Garrick was
still a wine-merchant, but with yearnings for the
stage. Anyhow, he, too, went to the Smock Alley
Theatre, and played with her there. When they
returned to Drury Lane, no secret was made of the
fact that they were lovers. They set up house at
No. 6, Bow Street, close by the theatre, together
with the well-known actor, Charles Macklin. This
" tripartite domestic arrangement " failed, as, of
course, it was bound to do ; and Garrick and Peg
went to live together in Southampton Street, Strand.
Alternatively, they paid the month's expenses ; and
their friends noted that when it was the actress's turn,
they were far better regaled. " I remember," Dr.
Johnson said, " drinking tea with David Garrick long
ago, when Peg made it, and he grumbled at her for
making it too strong." It was at one time believed
that Garrick intended to marry her, and she herself
told Arthur Murphy that he had gone so far as to

" try on " a wedding-ring. Whether this was ever in
Garrick's mind, no one can say. If it was, he probably
altered his intention, when he found that she was
unfaithful to him. Among her devoted admirers was
Owen MacSwinny, the playwright and theatrical
manager ; but he was so much her senior that it is
unlikely he was her lover. When he died in 1754,
being then considerably over seventy years of age, he
left her his small fortune. It has been said that one
of the conditions attached to the legacy was that the
actress should abandon the Roman Catholic faith in
which she had been brought up, and join the Church
of England ; but the story has not been substantiated.
Another admirer was the well-known wit and man
about town, Sir Charles Hanbury Williams, who
wooed her in verse :

> " Once more I'll tune the vocal shell
>   To hills and dales my passions tell,
>   A flame which time can never quell,
>   That burns for lovely Peggy.
>
> " Ye greater bards the lyre should hit,
>   For say what subject is more fit,
>   Than to record the sparkling wit
>   And bloom of lovely Peggy.
>
> " The sun first rising in the morn,
>   That paints the dew-bespangled thorn,
>   Does not so much the day adorn
>   As does my lovely Peggy.
>
> " And when in Thetis lap to rest,
>   He, streaks with gold the ruddy west,
>   He's not so beauteous as undressed
>   Appears my lovely Peggy.
>
> " Were she arrayed in rustic weed,
>   With her the bleating flocks I'd feed,
>   And pipe upon my oaken reed,
>   To please my lovely Peggy.

" With her a cottage would delight,
　　All's happy when she's in my sight,
　　But when she's gone it's endless night,
　　　　All's dark without my Peggy.

" The zephyr air the violet blows,
　　Or breathes upon the damask rose,
　　He does not half the sweets disclose
　　　　That does my lovely Peggy.

" I stole a kiss the other day,
　　And trust me, nought the truth I say,
　　The fragrant breath of blooming may,
　　　　Was not so sweet as Peggy.

" While bees from flower to flower shall rove,
　　And linnets warble through the grove,
　　Or stately swans the waters love,
　　　　So long shall I love Peggy.

" And when death, with his pointed dart,
　　Shall strike the blow that rives my heart,
　　My words shall be when I depart,
　　　　Adieu, my lovely Peggy."

When Peg Woffington came back to Dury Lane,
she, for the season of 1742–43, received :—

Salary, 7 guineas a week　　．　　．　　．　　．	£364
A clear benefit, say　．　　．　　．　　．　　．	130
Clothes　．　　．　　．　　．　　．　　．　　．	50
	£544

If at Drury Lane, Peg did not play all the parts
that she desired, it was because in the company were
Kitty Clive and Hannah Pritchard, who, also popular
favourites, took their share of them. However, her
contributions to the success of the theatre were by no
means negligible. In 1743, she created Charlotte in
Henry Fielding's *The Wedding Day* ; and in the
following season she appeared as Ophelia, Mrs. Ford,

Lady Townly, Portia in *The Merchant of Venice*, and Millamont in Congreve's *The Way of the World*.

Probably nothing in Peg Woffiington's career gave her more pleasure than, at her own benefit on April 30, 1745, the appearance, " for the first time on any stage," of her younger sister Mary in the part of Cherry in *The Beaux' Stratagem*. Peg, whatever her faults, looked after her family. She provided for her mother, and took Mary under her wing, and saw to it that she was properly educated. Mary was very pretty, and attracted many admirers. One was Captain the Honourable Robert Cholmondeley, who, when he left the Army, entered the Church, and became Rector of St. Andrew's, Hertford. He was the second son of George, third Earl of Cholmondeley, who had married in 1723, Mary, the only legitimate daughter of Sir Robert Walpole. Whatever her own morals, Peg was determined that no mischance should happen to her sister. However, Cholmondeley wanted to marry Mary, so all was well, except that the Earl was opposed to the alliance. Peg used all her fascination to charm his Lordship, and succeeded in inducing him to withdraw his opposition. When he yielded, he said to her that he had been " so very much offended previously " by the suggestion of the marriage. " Offended previously ! " said the actress, who, having had her way, was evidently in the most hoity-toity mood, " I have the most cause to be offended now." " Why, dear lady ? " she was asked. " Because," she retorted, " I had only one beggar to support, and now I shall have two ! " His Lordship's reply has not been recorded.

Mary was married to Robert Cholmondeley in 1746, in which year Horace Walpole wrote to Horace Mann : " I have been unfortunate in my own family. My

MARGARET WOFFINGTON AS PENELOPE
By Sir Joshua Reynolds

nephew, Captain Cholmondeley, has married a player's sister." If Peg had known of this remark, imagination boggles at what she would have retorted. There were several children of the marriage : Mary Henrietta, who was Maid of Honour to her Royal Highness the Princess of Wales, who, when driving with her mistress through Leatherhead in 1806, was killed by the overturning of the carriage ; Jane Elizabeth ; Hester Frances, who in 1783 married Sir William Bellingham, Bart.; Robert James ; and George James, who, born in 1752, became Receiver-General of Excise, which office he held until his death in 1830. Cholmondeley lived until 1804, and his wife survived for seven years.

The Honourable Mrs. Cholmondeley was not only attractive : she was intelligent, and moved much in literary and artistic circles. Just before his death, in 1774, Oliver Goldsmith showed her the manuscript of his *Retaliation*, which no one else but Edmund Burke had seen. She is mentioned in James Boswell's *Tour to the Hebrides*. Dr. Johnson described her as " a very airy lady " ; and there is an anecdote about her in Murphy's biography of the great man, which certainly indicates that she had a sense of humour : " Johnson, sitting at table with her, took hold of her hand in the middle of dinner, and held it close to his eye, wondering at the delicacy and the whiteness, till, with a smile she asked : ' Will he give it to me again when he has done with it ? ' " In 1775 she was at the house of Sir Joshua Reynolds, when, among the company, was Johnson, Boswell, and Dr. Samuel Musgrave, the editor of *Euripides*. In that year, Fanny Burney wrote : " Mrs. Cholmondeley has been praising *Evelina*. My father said that I could not have had a greater compliment than making two such

M

women my friends as Mrs. Thrale and Mrs. Cholmondeley, for they were severe, and afraid of praising
à tort et à travers, as their opinions are liable to be
quoted."

Garrick in 1747 entered into partnership with Lacy
at Dury Lane, reserving to himself the entire control
of the stage. He gathered together an excellent
company, Peg Woffington, Kitty Clive, Susannah
Maria Cibber, and Hannah Pritchard ; Macklin and
his wife ; Dennis Delane, Spranger Barry, Barrington,
Richard Yates, William Havard, Sparks, Mills, and
Lowe. Peg Woffington remained at Drury Lane until
the end of 1748, when she parted in a rage from
Garrick, who was making overtures to an Austrian
dancer, Eva Maria Violette, whom he married in the
following June.

Peg returned to Covent Garden, where Mrs. Cibber
and Spanger Barry had preceded her. Covent Garden
Theatre was not then a happy place. The " stars "
were at loggerheads with each other, and all of them,
or nearly all of them, with Mr. Manager Rich. Quin
and Barry disliked one another almost as much as
Mrs. Cibber disliked Peg Woffington. There was
jealousy on every side. Every now and then, for the
purpose of self-assertion, or through some passing fit
of jealousy, a member of this happy band would,
almost at the last moment, plead illness, and conse-
quent inability to act. The sympathies of the
audience went out to Rich, and when, after an
evening when Peg had disappointed them, she re-
appeared the next, she was greeted with cat-calls.
The lady was not dismayed. " She looked more
beautiful than ever," Genest has related. " Her
anger gave a glow to her complexion, and even added
lustre to her charming eyes. She behaved with great

resolution, and treated their rudeness with glorious contempt. She left the stage, and was called for, and, with infinite persuasion, was induced to return." It may well have been that Peg was upset ; anyhow, she quarrelled with Rich, and went to Dublin. Mr. Saxe-Wyndham, the historian of Covent Garden Theatre, thinks this may have been because she thought the manager had instigated the unruly demonstration. Dutton Cook, in *Hours with the Players*, suggests another reason : " She quitted Covent Garden in 1751 at the close of the season in high dudgeon. She was offended at the names of Quin, Barry, and Mrs. Cibber being printed in unusual size upon the playbills, which should have been devoted to the comedies in which she appeared."

Peg Woffington in 1751 went back to Dublin, being offered for the first season at the Smock Alley Theatre four hundred pounds, and for any subsequent ones double that amount. As by her performances in four stock plays she brought to the management no less than four thousand pounds, the remuneration, though very high for those days, was not out of proportion to her drawing capacity. Her success was again immediate, not only with the younger folk who had grown up during the nine years that had intervened since her last appearance there, but with all those who had then admired her. George Faulkner, the well-known bookseller and printer, was present at her first night, and in the next issue of his *Dublin Journal* printed an article about the actress :

" The celebrated Mrs. Woffington's performance in Smock Alley Theatre continues to draw the most crowded audiences hitherto known. Her elegant deportment at her first entrance is a prologue in her behalf. Her correct pronunciation is accompanied by the most just and graceful action. Her unaffected ease and vivacity in comedy, her majestic pathos in tragedy, shows her to be an exact imitation of Nature, without the least appearance of her handmaid, Art, though, at the same time, possessed and executed by that lady in the highest degree.

"These eminent qualities have so universally obtained for her the esteem and applause of all the tasteful and judicious in this city, that it may be said of her, in imitation of Cæsar's phrase, ' She came, was seen, and she triumphed.' "

Then follows a long eulogy in rhyme on her genius, which ends :

> " Hail, then, in whom united we behold
> Whatever graced the theatres of old.
> A form above description ; and a mind
> By judgment temperèd, and by wit refined.
> Cut off in beauty's prime, when Oldfield died,
> The Muses wept, and threw their harps aside ;
> But how assumed, the lyre amazed to see
> Her greatest beauties far outdone by thee."

The eulogy amused Benjamin Victor, who, among other things, was the Treasurer of the Smock Alley Theatre, and he wrote a letter to Mrs. Woffington :

" Madame, you have long been the subject of true praise, and have received many public instances of it from the admiring world : but the scribbling fools here offer it up so fulsome, that instead of incense, I dare say it is as offensive to you as the snuff of a candle —now, madam, if my praise proves the snuff of a wax candle, it will not at least not offend, and I shall have reason to be satisfied." (This simile is rather obscure, but the manager goes on triumphantly) : " The silly poet in *Faulkner's Journal*, on Saturday last, made me laugh : he made you the successor to the poor antiquated Mrs. Vanderbank (who often declared that in her youth she was the glory of the Irish stage), and concludes it one of your least excellencies to far outdo Mrs. Oldfield.

"I was one of the audience when Lady Townly made her first appearance in London; and since the death of that celebrated actress, Mrs. Oldfield, I have not seen a complete Lady Townly till last Monday night. You know, she was called *inimitable* in that character, by the author, Cibber, that great master of comedy; but, I dare say, even he will admit that epithet falsified by your performance.

"After your first appearance in tragedy in London, I had the favour of two letters from him, in the first he employed a whole sheet in your praise in *Andromache*. I had so great a prepossession of your good understanding, and his judgment, that I could easily give him credit, though I had known him long an admirer of your person.

"On Wednesday night last I was convinced that you are a most provoking creature (to use the laureate's phrase). You are not content with destroying all our females, but make even our heroes shrink before you. I take this opportunity of congratulation, and beg to remain, your most humble servant."

Peg Woffington was at the height of her fame, crowded houses were the order of the evening; and she was applauded to the echo, whether she played in comedy or tragedy. "At this time," Robert Hitchcock says in his *Historical View of the Irish Stage*, "the theatre was the fashionable resort of all ranks. Crowded every night with first characters in the kingdom, it was in reality a source of entertainment and instruction. Its exhibitions might grace a Greek or a Roman stage. Propriety, order, and decorum,

presided over the whole. Its professors were held in
the highest esteem, admitted into the first assemblies,
and treated with the utmost respect." Charles
Macklin, who had always been devoted to Peg, wrote
in the same strain : " It was at this era, that Woffington might have been said to have reached the acme
of her fame ; she was then in the bloom of her
person, accomplishments, and profession; highly distinguished for her wit and vivacity ; with a charm of
conversation that at once attracted the admiration of
the men and the envy of the women. Her company
off, was equally sought for as on the stage ; and
though she did not much admire the frivolity of her
own sex, and consequently did not mix much with
them, she was the delight of some of the gravest and
most scientific characters in Church and State."

There was started in London about 1709 a Beefsteak
Club, the provisadore of which was Dick Estcourt, the
actor, and one of the most popular of men. Estcourt,
however, died three years later, whereupon Steele
paid tribute to him in the *Spectator*. " I am very
sorry that I have at present a circumstance before me
which is of very great importance to all who have a
relish for gaiety, wit, mirth, or humour : I mean the
death of poor Dick Estcourt. I have been obliged to
him for so many hours of jollity, that it is but a small
recompense, though all I can give him, to pass a
moment or two in sadness for the loss of so agreeable
a man. Poor Estcourt ! Let the vain and proud be
at rest, thou wilt no more disturb their admiration
of their dear selves ; and thou art no longer to drudge
in raising the mirth of stupids, who know nothing
of thy merit, for thy maintenance." The Sublime
Society of Beefsteaks was brought into being in 1735
by John Rich, and met in a room at Covent Garden

Theatre every Saturday evening. The membership was distinguished, and included Hogarth and his father-in-law, Sir John Thornhill, John Wilkes, Lord Sandwich, Charles Churchill (for a while), Charles Price, Mr. Justice Welsh, Arthur Murphy, Garrick, Bubb Dodington (afterwards Lord Melcombe), and several others.

Thomas Sheridan, the manager of the Smock Alley Theatre, decided to start a Beefsteak Club in Dublin. He gave a dinner in the great room of the theatre to some fifty persons of distinction, and propounded his scheme. About thirty of those present enrolled themselves as members, and elected Peg Woffington as president—the only woman to be a member of the Club. " The reader will readily believe," Benjamin Victor says, " that a club where there were good accommodations, such a lovely president full of wit and spirits, and nothing to pay (for Sheridan appointed himself perpetual host), must soon grow remarkably fashionable." It would be thought that nothing could have been more harmless than these gatherings—and, indeed, harmless they were ; but political passion ran high at the time, and people declared that it was nothing more or less than a hot-bed of the supporters of the Court. " Our city of Dublin," Victor has written, " in the parliamentary winters used to be the assembly of all the people of figure and fortune in the kingdom, who have had nothing to do here these thirty years past, but the government business and pursuing their pleasures ; but this winter a very strange thing called patriotism has appeared, and as violent an opposition in the House of Commons as ever was known in England to the measures of the government, which has drove the whole people into the most outrageous spirit of party ever known in the

kingdom. The consequence will, I fear, be fatal to
many of these patriots, for the king will no doubt
support his viceroy, and all within the power of
government have lost their places and pensions—a
loss I dare say they will have leisure to be sorry for.
This you will suppose has been very detrimental to all
public diversions, and the theatre has greatly suffered
by these commotions."

The objection to the Club spread to objection to its
originator, and the public determined to avenge themselves upon him. The opportunity soon came. On
February, 1754, *Mahomet* was played, with Sheridan,
Peg Woffington, and West Digges in the cast. The
play contains diatribes against ministers of state and
Court favourites, and Digges, as Alcanor, delivered
the following lines :

> " If, ye powers divine !
>   Ye mark the movements of this nether world,
>   And bring them to account ?   Crush, crush those vipers,
>   Who, singled out by the community
>   To guard their rights, shall for a grasp of ore,
>   Or paltry office, sell them to the foe."

The audience burst out into thunders of applause,
and demanded that the passage should be repeated.
A few days later there was a riot in the theatre, and
fire was set to the building, which was partially
destroyed. A series of benefits was arranged for those
actors and actresses who were thrown out of employ ;
and the first was given under the patronage of the
Lord-Lieutenant, the Duke of Dorset and the Duchess
of Dorset, to Peg Woffington, in *Love for Love*, who was
this time well received by an audience, many of whom
were rather ashamed of themselves and not disposed
for further mischief.

The immediate result of the riot was the return to

England of Peg Woffington, and the retirement of the disgusted Thomas Sheridan, who issued the following dignified notice :

" Mr. Sheridan, lately manager of the Theatre Royal, thinks it necessary to acquaint the public that he has entirely quitted the stage, and will be no more concerned in the direction of it. He has lent the house to the performers during their benefits without any emolument to himself. He hoped to have been able before this time to have laid before the public a full vindication of his conduct, but a near domestic concern has so far affected for some days past that it was impossible for him to give that attention to the subject which it required. He hopes, however, to have it published soon, and in the meantime earnestly entreats of all candid and impartial persons that they will not give ear to the many stories and falsehoods which are industriously propagated to his prejudice. He makes no doubt of convincing all (who are to be convinced) that he has done nothing but what he ought to have done, and that he could not have acted otherwise consistent with the character of a good citizen or a good manager."

Peg Woffington left Dublin for Covent Garden, and remained at that theatre until her retirement. She was frequently ill, but would not disappoint her audiences. " I have often seen her on the stage," Victor says, " when she ought to have been in bed." Perhaps it was this ill-health that made her lose her temper with Tate Wilkinson, then a lad of eighteen.

Wilkinson obtained an introduction to Garrick, who engaged him for the following season at thirty shillings a week. The great man asked him for his imitation of Samuel Foote, and then he volunteered an imitation of Peg—at which Garrick laughed inordin-

ately. " I thought it very comical," he writes, " and
that the joke might not be lost, I laughed too ; but,
on the merriment ceasing, I perceived a concealed
third laughter, which greatly puzzled me, when on a
sudden a green cloth double door flew open, which I
found led to a little breakfast parlour, and discovered
a most elegant lady, no less a personage than Mrs.
Garrick, who had, it seems, been purposely posted
there for her secret opinion of my imitations. Mrs.
Garrick apologised for her rudeness and intrusion,
confessed she had taken possession of that snug spot
unobserved at the desire of Mr. Garrick, as from his
account of my imitations she expected to be much
gratified ; but when she heard the tones of Mrs.
Woffington, the ridicule was so strongly pointed that it
was not in her power to refrain from laughter by the
pleasure and great satisfaction she had received."

Of course, this—but goodness knows how—came to
the ears of Peg. One evening when she was playing
Clarina in *The Confederacy*, she approached the box
in which Wilkinson was sitting, looked at him in a
manner which made him shrink back, and finished her
speech in a sarcastic manner. " My unfortunate star
was then predominant," says Wilkinson, speaking of
this night, " for at that moment a woman of the town,
in the balcony above where I was seated, repeated
some words in a remarkably shrill tone, which occasioned a general laugh ; like electricity, it caught Mrs.
Woffington's ear, whose voice was far from being
enchanting on perceiving the pipe squeak on her right
hand, and being conscious of the insult she had then
given apparently to me, it struck her comprehension
so forcibly that she immediately concluded I had given
the retort upon her in that open and audacious
manner. She again turned and darted her lovely eyes,

though assisted by the furies, which made me look confounded and sheepish ; all of which only served to confirm my condemnation." The next day they met in Rich's room. Peg, coming out of the manager's room, passed him without a word ; then she turned, and addressed him in her best tragedy tones : " Mr. Wilkinson, I have made a visit to Mr. Rich, to insist on his not giving you any engagement, whatever. Your impudence to me last night, where you had with such assurance placed yourself, is one proof of your ignorance ; added to that, I heard you echo my voice when I was acting, and I sincerely hope, in whatever barn you are suffered as an unworthy stroller, that you will fully experience the same comtempt you dared last night to offer me." This was really hard on the lad, who, anyhow, was innocent of the second offence. " Without waiting, or permitting me to reply," he says, " she darted once more to her chair. I really was so astonished, frightened, and bewildered that I knew not how to act or think." It may be mentioned that when Wilkinson mimicked Garrick on his own stage he, always fearful of ridicule, was just as furious as Peg had been.

Foote, who had lampooned nearly everyone, heard that Rich proposed to put on his play *The Mirror*, at Covent Garden, in which the author had mimicked Whitford, the preacher, Longford, the auctioneer, and a lady of the town known as Mother Douglas. The rumour had reached Foote that he was to be mimicked in his own play, and, infuriated, he rushed to the theatre, and burst into the manager's room. " Damn it, you old hound," he shouted vigorously, " if you dare let Wilkinson, that pug-nosed dog, take any liberty with me as to mimicry, I will bring you your-self, Rich, on the stage. If you want to engage that

pug, black his face, and let him hand a tea-kettle in a
pantomime. If he dares to appear in my character in
The Minor, I will instantly produce your old, stupid,
ridiculous self, with your cats, and your hound of a
mimic, altogether next week at Drury Lane, for the
general diversion of the pit, boxes, and galleries ; and
that will be paying you, you squinting old Hecate, too
great a compliment." The performance did not take
place. " I believe," Wilkinson says, " Rich dreaded
an affront on his favourite cats more than on himself."

Peg's temper was perhaps never completely under
control, and her gusts of passion frightened her fellow-
players. For instance, she was very jealous of George
Anne Bellamy, who was at least as beautiful and
nearly a score of years younger. In the season of 1756,
while playing Roxana to her rival's Statira, she drove
her off the stage, and stabbed her almost in the sight
of the audience. It was around this lamentable
incident that Samuel Foote wrote his *Green Room
Squabble, or, a Battle Royal between the Queen of
Babylon and the Daughter of Darius.* So, too, did
Peg hate Kitty Clive—" no two women ever hated
each other more," Davies, the biographer of Garrick,
noted.

Peg Woffington played the usual round of comedy
parts during these last years—Lady Townly in *The
Provoked Husband*, Lady Betty Modish in Colley
Cibber's *The Careless Husband*, Mrs. Sullen in *The
Beaux' Stratagem*, Angelina in *Love Makes a Many*;
and, as a contrast, the Queen in *Hamlet*.

Her last performance was on May 3, 1757. She was
playing Rosalind in *As You Like It*, and was taken
ill, but contrived to carry on to the end. However,
when she was delivering the Epilogue, she got so far

as the words, " If I were among you, I'd kiss as many of you as had beards that pleased me . . ." and then broke down, and was led off the stage by Tate Wilkinson, who says : " The audience, of course, applauded until she was out of sight, and then sunk into awful looks at seeing a favourite actress struck so suddenly by the hand of death (for so it seemed) in such a situation and in her prime of life. She was that night given over, and for several days ; but she so far recovered as to linger till 1760, but as a mere skeleton."

" What has become of Mrs. Woffington ? " someone enquired soon after. " She has been taken off by Colonel Cæsar," another replied. " Reduced to *aut Cæsar aut nullus*," said Lord Tyrawley.

" She is gone to be married," interjected Kitty Clive ; " Colonel Cæsar bought the licence at the same time Colonel Mostyn bought his."

As a matter of fact, Peg Woffiington was at the time living under the protection of Colonel Cæsar, to whom, it was believed by many, she was secretly married. She lived with him at Teddington ; but went back to her house in Vincent Square, Westminster, early in 1760, where she died on March 28 in that year.

Peg Woffington has been immortalised on the stage in *Masks and Faces*, by Tom Taylor and Charles Reade, and in Charles Reade's novel, based upon the play, that has her name as its title. Reade idealised her, and not to do so is difficult indeed, for her charm is indisputable. Not only was she generous to a fault, but she was thoughtful and considerate, and not all the adulation she received from all ranks of society could spoil her simple generous nature. " To her honour be it ever remembered," Hitchcock paid tribute, " that whilst in the zenith of her glory,

courted and caressed by all ranks and degrees, it made
no alteration in her behaviour : she remained the same
gay, affable, obliging, good-natured Woffington to
everyone around her. Not the lowest performer in the
theatre did she refuse playing for. Out of twenty-six
benefits in one season, she acted in twenty-four. Such
traits of character must endear the memory of Mrs.
Woffington to every lover of the drama." One of her
last acts was to ask George Anne Bellamy, with whom
she had quarrelled, to come to see her on her death-
bed. George Anne came, and they were reconciled.
Probably this was the only enemy she ever had—even
Tate Wilkinson could not quarrel with her.

Her amours, as has been said, were numerous, but
her contemporaries agreed with Arthur Murphy,
when he credited her with, " honour, truth, benevo-
lence, and charity."

John Hoole wrote a " Monody on the Death of Mrs.
Woffington," which concludes :

> " Whene'er we view'd the Roman's sullied fame,
> Thy beauty justified the hero's shame.
> What heart but then must Anthony approve,
> And own the world was nobly lost for love ?
> What ears could hear in vain thy cause implor'd,
> When soothing arts appeased thy angry lord ?
> Each tender breast the rough Ventidious blam'd,
> And Egypt gain'd the sigh Octavia claim'd.
> Thy eloquence each hush'd attention drew,
> While love usurp'd the tears to virtue due.
> See Phædra rise majestic o'er the scene !
> What raging pangs distract the hapless Queen !
> How does thy sense the poet's thought refine,
> Beam thro' each word, and brighten every line ;
> What nerve, what vigour, glows in every part,
> While classic lays appear with classic art !
> Who now can bid the proud Roxana rise,
> With love and anger sparkling in her eyes ?

Who now shall bid her beast in fury glow
With all the semblance of Imperial woe ?
While the big passion raging in her veins,
Would hold the master of the world in chains.
But Alexander now forsakes our coast,
And ah ! Roxana is for ever lost !

" Nor less thy power, when rigid virtue fir'd
The chaster bard and purer thought inspir'd ;
What kneeling form appears with steadfast eye,
Her bosom heaving with devotion's sigh ?
'Tis she ! in thee we own the mournful scene,
The fair semblance of a martyr Queen !
Here Guido's skill might mark thy speaking frame,
And catch from thee the painter's magic flame !

" Blest in each art ! by Nature's form'd to please,
With beauty, sense, with eloquence and ease !
Whose piercing genius studied all mankind,
All Shakespeare opening to thy vig'rous mind.
In every sense of comic humour known,
In sprightly sallies, with was all thine own,
Whether you seem'd the city's more humble wife,
Or shone in Townly's higher sphere of life.
A Proteus still, in all the varying range,
Thyself the same, divine in every change."

SUSANNAH MARIA CIBBER (*née* ARNE)
1714–1766

SUSANNAH MARIA CIBBER
(née ARNE)
1714–1766

"HER great excellence consisted in that simplicity which needed no ornament; in that sensibility which despised all art. There was in her countenance a small share of beauty; but Nature had given her such symmetry of form and fine expression of feature that she preserved all the appearance of youth long after she had reached to middle life. The harmony of her voice was as powerful as the animation of her look. In grief or tenderness her eyes looked as if they were in tears; in rage and despair they seemed to dart flashes of fire. In spite of the unimportance of her figure, she maintained a dignity in her action and a grace in her step."

Thus Thomas Davies in his *Life of David Garrick*, on Susannah Maria Cibber, and a very handsome tribute it is.

Susannah Maria was the daughter of one Arne, an upholsterer working in Covent Garden, who was the original of the political upholsterer immortalised by Addison in the *Tatler*, as "who, in his concern for the affairs of Europe, neglected his own business."

Susannah Maria was born in February 1714, about four years after her brother, Thomas Augustine, the famous musical conductor. At this time, the father was still fairly well-to-do, and gave his children a

good education. They both had musical gifts, which
the fond parent was at pains to cultivate. Of the
girl's earlier years, there is no record. In fact, there
is nothing of interest known about her until at the
age of eighteen she made her first appearance in
public as a singer at the theatre in the Haymarket as
the heroine in Lumpé's opera, *Amelia*, when she
scored a success. She continued to play in opera,
steadily increasing her reputation until 1736, when
she decided to become an actress on the " legitimate "
stage.

Two years earlier, she had married Theophilus, a
son of Colley Cibber, who was eleven years her senior—
according to Benjamin Victor, "very much against her
will"; though as to what urged her to this marriage,
he gives no clue. Victor describes the husband as
"then not long a widower, of small stature, and of
extravagant and vicious habits."

Cibber certainly was from the first an unsatisfactory
husband. His redeeming quality was a sense of
humour. When in May 1722 Theophilus Cibber took
his benefit—the play was *Richard III*—he announced
it " for the entertainment of those who will come."
Sometimes, Doran tells us, Theophilus advertised his
benefit as being for himself and creditors jointly ;
and in April 1746 he, a comedian of the first rank,
thus appealed to the consideration of the public :
" As I have, in justice to my creditors, assigned over
as much of my salary as reduces the remainder to a
very small pittance, I very much depend on the indulgence and encouragement of the town at my
benefit, whose favours shall be gratefully remembered
by their very humble servant, Theophilus Cibber."
On these occasions, the beneficiary sometimes made
merry. James Spiller in 1720 advertised a perform-

ance at the theatre in Lincoln's Inn Fields, "for the benefit of himself and creditors." "I think," says this one-eyed comedian, "I have found out what will please the multitude. I have tolerably good luck, and tickets rise apace, which makes mankind very civil to me, for I get up every morning to a levée of at least a dozen people, who pay their compliments, and ask the same question, ' When shall we be paid ? ' All I can say is, wicked good company has brought me into this imitation of grandeur. I loved my friend and my jest too well to grow rich : in short, wit," says the comedian, sporting with his own infirmity, " is my blind side." Even more amusing was the announcement of George Lillo, author of the famous tragedy, *The London Merchant, or, The History of George Barnwell*, that the third, or author's night of his *Elmeric* would be given for " the benefit of my poor relations."

Early in 1738, Cibber had to fly the country in order to be out of the reach of his creditors. When he returned in the winter of that year, he brought an action against a Mr. Sloper, for " criminal conversation with his wife." The general impression was that he had deliberately thrown her in Sloper's way, with a view to obtaining damages. In this, he was sadly disappointed, for he claimed damages to the amount of £5000 ; and the jury awarded him £5—thus very definitely expressing their opinion of his connivance. In the following year, he brought another action, asking for £10,000. This time he was given £500.

Susannah Maria never returned to her husband, but lived with Sloper at his house, Woodhays, where she was visited by, among others, the Garricks.

About this time, Theophilus Cibber, then only in the late 'thirties, conceived the idea of writing his autobiography, and actually went so far as to solicit subscriptions. Some malicious fellow—there are those who suspect no less a person than Henry Fielding—published in 1740 what has been described as " a caustic review of a not too reputable career," under the title of " An Apology for the Life of Mr. The' Cibber, Comedian. Being a Proper Sequel to the Apology for the Life of Mr. Colley Cibber, Comedian, with an Historical View of the Stage to the Present Year. Supposed to be written by Himself in the Style and Manner of the Poet Laureat." Consequently, Theophilus' autobiography never appeared.

The reports of the two cases are sufficiently interesting to be given here.

THE TRIAL FOR CRIMINAL CONVERSATION

On Thursday, the 5th of December, 1738, at nine o'clock in the morning, at the sitting of the Court of King's Bench, in Middlesex, before the Right Hon. Sir William Lee, Knt., Lord Chief Justice, of that Court, came on the remarkable trial before a special jury of gentlemen, of a cause in which Theophilus Cibber, Gent., was the Plaintiff, and William Sloper, Esq., was Defendant.

The Declaration (which was opened by the Junior Counsel for the Plaintiff) was for Assaulting, Ravishing, and Carnally Knowing Susannah Maria Cibber, the Plaintiff's wife ; and this was laid to be done at several periods of time, as divers days, between such a day, to such a day, at each period. Whereby (the Declaration said) the Plaintiff lost the Company, Comfort, Society, Assistance, etc., of his wife to his damage of FIVE THOUSAND POUNDS.

The Counsel for the Plaintiff were Mr. Solicitor-General, Mr. Hollings, Sergeant Agar, Mr. Marsh,

Mr. Dennison, and Mr. Lawson; and the Counsel for Defendant were Sergeant Eyre, Mr. Noel, Mr. Lloyd, Mr. Murray, and Mr. Barnardiston.

It is here proper to let the reader understand that this trial is not taken in the very words at length, as is sometimes done when shorthand writers can be conveniently placed. But the person who attended on this occasion was at such disadvantages that he was forced to take it in an abridged way, writing down the substance of it as well as he could. We thought good to mention this, that we may not be understood to impose on our readers, nor to injure the great men concerned. We therefore hope that neither the learned gentlemen at the Bar nor the Court will be offended that we cannot do them full justice in printing at length the very good arguments on both sides, and his Lordship's excellent charge to the jury.

Mr. Solicitor-General (John Strange, Esq.) stated the case for the Plaintiff, and (among many other things) observed to the Court and the Jury that the injury done to the Plaintiff was of the most tender concern to his peace of mind, happiness, hopes of prosperity, and was the highest of all injuries for which he came before them to seek a recompense or satisfaction in damages, and that indeed it was impossible to give a pecuniary satisfaction adequate to the injury, for that no sum of money could restore a man's tranquillity of mind, but that the Plaintiff must rest upon such remedy as the law had given him.

He further observed (upon the Plaintiff's being a Player) that 'tis true the Plaintiff was a Player, but he was also a gentleman, being well descended and having a liberal education; that the Plaintiff himself was a good Player, and that his father was well-known to all gentlemen who delighted in theatrical entertainments to be of the first figure in that profession, and an author too, and the Plaintiff's grandfather was the best Statuary of his time; and that the Plaintiff, by the mother's side, was related to William of Wickham, and in right of that pedigree had received his education upon a foundation of that great man.

He said he knew it was attempted by some to have the Players considered in a matter of this nature as not upon the same footing with the rest of the subjects, as if it were more lawful to invade their properties than those of other people; but he knew no law that deprived them of those comforts, or of those rights, which other subjects ought to enjoy. That the Stage had been cherished and encouraged by the wisest statesmen as a school of virtue and good morals, and that many receive good lessons and impressions from what they hear at the Theatre, who perhaps don't incline to go seek for instruction elsewhere.

That there had been a good deal of pains to spread a report about town as if the Plaintiff had been consenting to the wrong the Defendant had done him; but this was only to lose the credit of the Plaintiff's cause before the trial, and that it might come with prejudice before the Jury. That his brief instructed him that there could not be the least colour or shadow of proof to support such a surmise.

Mr. Solicitor-General also stated the evidence for the Plaintiff, in part as it comes from the Plaintiff's witnesses in the following pages, but as to part of what comes from Mr. Carter, of Kensington, it doubtless was never mentioned in his brief. As to the

SUSANNAH MARIA CIBBER
After T. Hudson

principal facts he mentioned the witness, Mr. Hayes, looking through a hole in a wainscot partition, which parted Mr. Hayes's closet from a room in which the Defendant and Mrs. Cibber were together, and that through the hole Mr. Hayes, at several different days and times, saw them guilty of criminal familiarities, and in such acts, and with such circumstances, and particularly the last time, he (Mr. Hayes) saw such a sight as he (Mr. Solicitor) would leave to the witness to tell, for it ought to be related but once.

Mr. Hollings spoke very well on the same side, pathetically observing to the Gentlemen of the Jury, the mischievous consequences of suffering a man to commit such an injury to the married state without being obliged to repair it in damages, that the Plaintiff was an Englishman, and as such, had rights which ought not to be invaded, particularly in the present instance, that he had brought his case before a Jury of English gentlemen, and he (Mr. Hollings) did not doubt that they would give the Plaintiff proper damages.

The Plaintiff's Counsel then proceeded to call their witnesses ; and first to prove the marriage between the Plaintiff and his wife, they called Mrs. Brett, but she did not appear at this time.[1]

The Plaintiff's Attorney then named Mr. Cibber, the Plaintiff's father, who, being present in Court, was sworn. His evidence was in substance as follows :

Q. Do you know of the Plaintiff's being married to his present wife ?

[1] She appeared in the afternoon, as will be mentioned hereafter.

MR. CIBBER. I was not at the marriage, but I am as well convinced that they were married, as that I myself was married. I was against the match.

Q. Why were you against the match?

MR. CIBBER. Because she had no fortune.

Q. Did they at first live happily together?

MR. CIBBER. They did live happy, very happy, much happier than I expected, as I was always adverse to the match.

Q. How long did they thus live happily together?

MR. CIBBER. About three years. Within that time they had two children, which are both dead.

Q. Did Mr. Cibber, the Plaintiff, during that time support her well and liberally, as became an affectionate husband?

MR. CIBBER. He did, even to profusion. I often admonished him about it, and advised to retrench his expenses, for I thought them a good deal too large for his condition, or what he was able to afford. He made her several valuable presents of rings and jewels.

Q. Is not Mrs. Cibber a good actress, and how did she become so?

MR. CIBBER. When they were married she was a singer, but there were better voices. I thought her voice not the best, and if not best, it's nothing. I thought it might possibly do better for speaking. I asked her husband if he had ever heard her speak a part; he said he had, and that she did it very prettily. I tried her, and was surprised to find her do it so very well.

Q. Did not her husband take pains to instruct her?

MR. CIBBER. I believe I was the person who chiefly instructed her. I spent a good deal of time, and took great delight in it, for she was very capable of receiving instruction. In forty years' experience that I have known the stage, I never knew a woman at the beginning so capable of the business, or improve so fast.

Q. When did you first hear of any disagreement in the family ?

MR. CIBBER. Soon after he came from France, about last April.

MR. FLEETWOOD, Master of Drury Lane Playhouse, was sworn.

Q. Sir, do you know the Plaintiff's wife ? Is she a good player ?

MR. FLEETWOOD. Yes, Sir, I think her a good player for her time.

Q. What salary did you give her ? What advantages did she bring to her husband ?

MR. FLEETWOOD. She played three seasons. For the first her salary was an hundred pounds, and she had a benefit.

Q. What was the benefit worth ?

MR. FLEETWOOD. I can't be particular, because I have not looked into the accounts on this occasion. If I had known I should have been examined as to this, I could have been particular. I believe it might be a hundred pounds.

Q. Well, Sir, the second year ?

MR. FLEETWOOD. That must have been a good deal better than an hundred pounds.

Q. Then the third year ?

MR. FLEETWOOD. Her salary the third year was two hundred pounds, and she had a benefit.

Q. What was that worth ?

MR. FLEETWOOD. I believe it must have been worth an hundred and fifty pounds, for she grew much in the favour of the town, and 'twas a very good benefit.[1]

Q. Sir, how comes it that Mrs. Cibber does not play this season ?

MR. FLEETWOOD. Because we could not agree upon the terms. I would not come up to her terms.

Q. What were her terms ?

MR. FLEETWWOOD. She insisted to have as good a salary as any woman in the house, and the first benefit.

Q. Perhaps she deserves as much ; is she not as good a player as any in the house ?

MR. FLEETWOOD. I can't say that, I can't pretend to determine that. I have got more money by Mrs. Clive,

Mr. Quin, Mr. Johnson, and some others were called for this purpose, but the Court was of opinion 'twas now proper for the Plaintiff's Counsel to establish their principal fact.

MRS. HAYES was then sworn.

Q. Mrs. Hayes, pray give my Lord and the Jury an account of the Defendant's and Mrs. Cibber's coming to your house. Do you know Mrs. Hopson ?

MRS. HAYES. Yes, sir, it was just this day twelve months, the fifth of December, that Mrs. Hopson came into my lodgings. I lived in Blue Cross Street,

[1] The examination to these matters was at first opposed by the Defendant's Counsel as not being supported by the Declaration; but the Plaintiff's Counsel insisted that it being laid in the Declaration, that by the means there alleged, the Plaintiff had lost the assistance of his wife, he had a right to prove the loss he had sustained by the Defendant's taking her off the stage, and the *quantum* of that loss. And of what opinion was the Court, so Mr. Fleetwood was examined as above. The Defendant's Counsel insisted that nothing here appeared that the Defendant had taken her off the stage, and they cross-examined Mr. Fleetwood.

Leicester Fields. On the Saturday Mrs. Hopson
came to my house and took my lodgings. She beat
them down as low as she could, for she said she was a
single woman, and should give but little trouble;
she had nobody to come after her, but a lady and a
gentleman that would come to see her sometimes.
She had the lodgings for seven shillings a week; two
rooms on the first floor. There was a bed in each of
them. One of the beds was a turn-up bed. She was
to come in on Sunday; but she sent me word that she
should not come in till Monday, and on Monday, the
fifth of December, she came in a hackney-coach, and
some boxes and some things with her. On Sunday
evening, a young gentleman, whom I afterwards knew
to be Mr. Sloper, called and asked if Mrs. Hopson
had not taken the lodgings, and whether she was
come. We told him that she had taken the lodgings,
but that she had sent word she should not come till
Monday.

She lay there on Monday night. Neither Mrs.
Cibber nor Mr. Sloper came that day, but they came
soon after—I think it was on a Tuesday—and they
supped together, and went away between eleven and
twelve o'clock. Mrs. Hopson sat up and let them out,
and locked the door after them. They often came in the
space of six weeks that Mrs. Hopson had the lodgings
—I believe near twenty times. They did not come
together, but dropped in one after the other. They
sometimes dined, but most commonly supped, there.
Mrs. Hopson used to leave them together every time
they came; sometimes an hour, sometimes two or
three hours at a time. She often made errands to go
out to buy something, and sometimes sat two hours
at a time below stairs with me, while they were above
together. They stayed sometimes till one or two

o'clock in the morning, and how they went away I cannot tell, for I was in bed at these times, but I believe they usually went in chairs or coaches.

Q. When they were alone did they use to fasten the door ?

MRS. HAYES. Yes, the door used to be fast. Mrs. Hopson used to go and knock at it, and they let her in ; and sometimes she could not get in, and used to come downstairs again.

Q. How did you know they were Mr. Sloper and Mrs. Cibber ?

MRS. HAYES. There was an acquaintance of mine at my house one day when Mrs. Hopson came down stairs to me, one Mr. Rowe, and he knew Mrs. Hopson. " How do you do, Mrs. Hopson ? " said he ; so after she was gone, I asked him who Mrs. Hopson was, and he told me she was Mrs. Cibber's maid ; so I gave her warning, and let my lodgings to another, for I did not like their coming. Mrs. Hopson did not usually lie there o' nights, except when they had been there in the evening, but on those nights she lie there. One day after I gave her warning, Mr. Sloper was in a great passion above-stairs at something, and Mrs. Hopson came to me. " You have made a fine kettle of fish of it," says she. I did not know what she meant by her kettle of fish. " What fish do you mean ? " says I. " Why, there," says she, " you have been talking of matters, and he's stark mad of it above stairs." She would have kept the lodgings, but I chose not ; I let them to another, and so they went away.

Q. Did Mr. Cibber ever call at your house and talk with you about them ?

MRS. HAYES. Yes, about five or six months ago he came and asked me if Mrs. Hopson had not lodged there. I told him she had. He asked who came to see her, and I described them, both by their clothes and their persons ; so he said no more, and went away.

MR. HAYES sworn.

Q. Sir, give an account of Mrs. Hopson's lodging at your house, and who came to see her, and what happened.

MR. HAYES. When Mrs. Hopson had my lodgings, Mr. Sloper and Mrs. Cibber came often to her, and she used to leave them together two or three hours at a time. They used to go away at one, two, or three o'clock in the morning in coaches or chairs. I have a closet on the same floor, adjoining to the room where they used to sit ; I bored holes through the wainscot, and could see them very plain. He used to kiss her, and take her on his lap. On the twelfth day of January I was locked up in the closet at one o'clock in the afternoon, and he came first, and he was angry because she was not at home, and sent Mrs. Hopson for her. In about two hours she came. Mrs. Hopson went away and left them alone ; so he spoke something to her in an angry way about Mr. Fleetwood. She said she would take away his brother from his house, and that she did not value Mr. Fleetwood. He and she grew friends again, and they made it up, and he took her upon his lap.

Hereupon some further questions were offered as to the fact. His Lordship interposed to this effect : " There is no occasion to be more particular ; we are not trying a rape." However, the witness did say there was a criminal conversation ; and being a foreigner, he expressed himself as much by gesture as by words.

Q. Was their chamber locked ?

MR. HAYES. No, it was fastened by a screw. The holes are there to be seen in the wainscot and the door.

Q. Whom did the screw belong to ?

MR. HAYES. I believe it was Mrs. Hopson's. I have seen it lying in the chamber window.

Q. How did you know who they were ?

MR. HAYES. Mr. Rowe was one day at our house, and he spoke to Mrs. Hopson, and afterwards he said she was Mrs. Cibber's maid. Besides, I dogged them both home in their chairs. Her chair carried her to Mr. Cibber's house, No. 12, in Little Wild Court, and his chair went to his father's house in St. James's Place. After he was gone into the house I asked the chairman whose house that was, and they told me old Mr. Sloper's. I had often seen him at the tennis-court, and knew his name there.

Mr. Rowe was sworn.

MR. ROWE. I was one day at Mr. Hayes's, and Mrs. Hopson came in. I asked how she did. I had known her for a good many years before ; and the last time I had seen her I had been told she lived with Mr. Cibber. I believe I told Mr. Hayes so.

JURYMAN. My Lord, we would beg leave to call back the last witness (Mr. Hayes), to ask him this question—Why he took the pains to dog Mr. Sloper's chair at that time of night, to learn who he was, when he had known him before at the tennis-court.

MR. HAYES being called in again, and the question put to him he answered to this purpose : " As Mr. Sloper and Mrs. Cibber came into my house I knew them both, because I had seen him at the tennis-court, and her on the stage ; but to be more certain, I went and followed their chairs, as I told you."

MR. CARTER was sworn.

Q. Give an account of Mr. Cibber and Mrs. Cibber's lodging at your house in March last, and whether Mr. Sloper resorted there.

Mr. Carter. Yes, Sir, on the second of March Mrs. Cibber took the lodgings. I believe for them all there were three beds.

Q. Do you remember anything of Mr. Cibber's going to France, and whether Mr. Sloper came there during his absence.

Mr. Carter. Yes. Mr. Cibber went to France soon after, and Mr. Sloper did lodge there part of the time while he was absent, and he lodged there again soon after Mr. Cibber came back, and there was a lodging taken for Mr. Cibber at Blue Green, about a mile and a half from Kensington, and afterwards Mr. Cibber, Mrs. Cibber, and Mr. Sloper had supped together. Mr. Cibber had a man with a lanthorn and a candle, between nine and ten o'clock at night, to light him to Blue Green. He came back to breakfast next morning, and every morning, and they dined and sometimes supped together, and he went to Blue Green at night, and Mr. Sloper and Mrs. Cibber lay at my house, but I do not know what beds they lay in. When Mr. Sloper went away from my house back to London, Mr. Cibber left Blue Green and came and lay at my house.

Q. Who bore the expense of their housekeeping ?

Mr. Carter. Mr. Sloper did. Sometimes he gave my wife money to lay out, at other times my wife laid out what was necessary, and made a bill of it, and Mr. Sloper paid it.

Q. Did Mr. Cibber know this ?

Mr. Carter. Yes, Sir, it was very often before his face.

Q. Did he offer to pay anything ?

Mr. Carter. No, Sir.

Hannah Calcot and Ruth Calcot, being severally sworn and examined, had little to say.

o

They lived at Burnham in Buckinghamshire, where Mr. Sloper and Mrs. Cibber spent part of last summer. They did not live in the family. The amount of their evidence was, that Mr. Sloper and Mrs. Cibber lived at the same house at Burnham ; they were sure he lived there, because they had seen him walk abroad in his slippers, and in an undress.

FIFE and WATSON being severally sworn (Mr. Fife, 'tis said, is a Sergeant in the Guards), deposed, that they and another in a coach went with Mr. Cibber to Burnham, in September last, to take away Mrs. Cibber ; that they left the coach in a field, and went to the house, where she and Mr. Sloper were ; that she was in a night-gown sitting at the tea-table, and Mr. Sloper was at the other side of it, in his slippers ; and that Mr. Cibber said he come to demand his wife ; and that Mr. Sloper cursed and swore, and called Mr. Cibber hard names, but suffered one of the witnesses to lead her to the coach, and walked on the other side of her himself ; that she gave him a watch out of her pocket, on which he said, " By G——, well remembered ; the rascal would have had it else." That they drove away with Mrs. Cibber in the coach, along with Mr. Cibber and two of his assistants, the third being on horseback. That Mr. Sloper soon overtook them ; that he was booted and on horseback ; that he swore there was a villain in that coach, who should never live to go into another. They came to Slough ; and there, Mrs. Cibber not being well, desired Mr. Sloper (who was at the side of the coach, before the door of the inn) to get her a dram, and that Mr. Sloper brought her a glass of rum. She was about a quarter of an hour in the coach at the door of the inn, while Mr. Cibber was in the house providing for her accommodation. That when Mr. Cibber was in

the chamber of the inn, she called her husband a
great many villains, and said that now he had ruined
her reputation, she did not value it if all the world
knew that she was with child by Squire Sloper, and
that she loved him dearly, for he was an honourable
gentleman ; that Mr. Sloper took up a room in the inn
for some time, swore much, and fired a pistol, which
one of the witnesses seemed to believe was intended
at him, but cross-examined, he did own that the
muzzle was elevated, so as to point over the stable ;
and also that Mr. Cibber and his assistants had
two cases of pistols loaded. These proved that Mr.
Sloper went away in the night-time from the inn,
which determined Mr. Cibber to stay all night ;
that he sat up all night himself, and procured a woman
to lie in the bed with his wife. She would eat no supper
though there was one provided, for she was sulky.
The next day he did not take the direct road to London,
but drove across part of the country, and go to
London in the evening.

STINT was sworn.

STINT. (We hear that Mr. Stint is a candle-snuffer
at the playhouse.) Mr. Cibber employed me to take
care of his wife when he brought her to town, that
she might not be taken away again, and he used her
and provided for her very honourably, and gave orders
at the tavern, the Bull's Head, near Clare Market,
that she should want for nothing ; meat was dressed
there for her, and brought to her, and wine, a pint
of white and a pint of red. She complained that it
was cold weather, and I made her a fire, and locked
her up in the room, but she knocked and called,
and begged for God's sake I would let her out, or
else she would be stifled, for the chimney smoked.
So I let her out, and put out the fire. Mr. Thomas

Arne, her brother, came there, and he begged and
prayed that I would let her go along with him, but
I would not break my trust—I could not do it.   He
came several times, and finding I would not do it,
began to break open the house, and at the same time
bid her cry out murder.   She cried out murder,
and I believe there was a hundred of a mob assisting
him to break open the house.   I had a case of pistols,
and laid my back against the door, but they were too
strong for me, and took my pistols out of each hand
and held me fast by each arm, and beat me severely,
and tore all the clothes off my back, and took Mrs.
Cibber away with them.

APPLESFORD, the Reading Stage Coachman, was
sworn.

The witness proved that he was hired to carry two
ladies and a gentleman, sometime in September last,
from Slough to Reading.   He was to meet them at
Slough, and met them accordingly.   The gentleman
walked out of town in his boots, about half an hour
before the coach, and when the witness overtook
him, he took him in.   He knew neither him nor the
women.

The witness was paid two guineas for his charges,
and several other witnesses from Slough were also
paid who had nothing to say to the purpose.

MRS. BRETT was sworn.

She proved the marriage ; and being asked when
and where she saw Mrs. Cibber last, she answered,
this morning at her mother's.

This last question was asked because it had been
insinuated that Mrs. Cibber at that very time co-
habited with Mr. Sloper.

MR. SERGEANT EYRE, for the Defendant, opened the
Defence.   And among other things observed, that he

believed this was the first action of that kind that
ever came from the theatre ; that he never heard
that it was a place celebrated for virtue ; that Mr.
Solicitor-General had taken some pains to display
the Plaintiff's pedigree as descended from William of
Wickham, who was a clergyman, celibacy prevailed
among the clergy ; therefore the Plaintiff could not
be descended in a right line from him. That love is
the most governing passion in human nature ; that
as it is so, all theatrical plays abound in it ; that they
cannot expect to please without it. That a very wise
and modest man, who hath wrote one of the best
plays extant, could not depend on his hero for success ;
that he was forced to interlard it with love scenes
or it might probably have been damned the first night ;
and this is the tragedy of *Cato*. That the hero of this
piece, that very Cato, the greatest man of the time he
lived in, is recorded in history to have had very free
notions of love and matrimony ; that he sent his wife
to breed out of her, and when they had done, he took
her back again very well contented. That the players
are a people who act and enter into all manner of
characters ; that their men and women are made to
fall in love with each other, this day with one, to-
morrow with another ; that this practice in variety
must give them an uncommon propensity to love
without any confinement of the passion to a particular
subject ; 'tis very likely that this enters into their
common course of life. That their women learn all
the allurements that can engage the eye and ear, and
strike the imagination of young gentlemen ; they
dress, chat, sing, dance and charm unguarded young
gentlemen, who are not aware of any ill-consequences.
That it had already appeared, and would further appear in the course of evidence, that if there was a

suspicion of anything amiss in the acquaintance between Mr. Sloper and Mrs. Cibber, that the Plaintiff must thank himself for it. That the Plaintiff had taken pains to bring them acquainted, to live under the same roof, and used to leave them together to improve their acquaintance. That he (Sergeant Eyre) hoped that nothing criminal had passed between them, but if there had, the Plaintiff had certainly encouraged it, and had no pretence to come to a Jury for damages.

Mr. Lloyd, on the same side, made an excellent speech, which we do not take upon us to give the reader; we shall only mention a hint or two. He hoped (as Mr. Sergeant Eyre had done) that nothing criminal had passed between the Defendant and the Plaintiff's wife; but if anything seemed to tend that way, it at the same time appeared that the Plaintiff was privy and consenting to whatever intercourse or familiarities there passed between them. That if there had been anything done amiss with such circumstances he submitted to his Lordship's direction, but apprehended that the Plaintiff had no wrong done him, upon this maxim in law and reason, *Volenti non fit injuria;* and that, therefore, he (the Plaintiff) ought not to have a verdict. But if it should be thought proper (notwithstanding such consent) to find a verdict for the Plaintiff, it would at least be fit and necessary for the Gentlemen of the Jury to proportion it to the size of the trespass, which he hoped would be taken into consideration upon this occasion.

He said this, and much more, in a much better manner than we can relate it (for a reason already given) and proceeded to the evidence for the Defendant.

ANNE HOPSON was sworn.

Q. Did you lodge at Mr. Hayes's about this time twelvemonth ?

ANNE HOPSON : Yes, sir. I was then out of service. I had left Mr. Cibber's, and I intended to follow the business of mantua-making. I was bred to it.

Q. Did Mr. Sloper and Mrs. Cibber sometimes meet at your lodgings ?

ANNE HOPSON. Yes, they came to see me pretty often. They desired they might come there, and usually had a bit of something for supper.

Q. For what purpose did they meet ?

ANNE HOPSON. As they were acquaintance, to converse together.

Q. Did you use to go out and leave them alone together ?

ANNE HOPSON. Yes, I often had occasion to go and buy something for supper, or some tea and sugar ; and I had occasion to be below stairs to get supper ready.

Q. When you came upstairs did you use to find the chamber door fast ?

ANNE HOPSON : Sometimes it was so, and Mr. Sloper used to open it to me.

Q. Pray, what could you believe was the occasion of these private meetings ?

ANNE HOPSON : I will tell you all I know of the matter. I do not fear my character—there are enough in Court that will give me a very good character. It was about March twelvemonth that Mr. Sloper used first to come to our house, to Mr. Cibber's. The servants did not know who he was, but my master called him Mr. Benefit, and used to say he was a romp, and a good-natured boy. Mr. Cibber was then very bare of money, and afraid of his creditors. I was very sorry for it, for he owed me a good deal of money, and does so still. But one day he told me, "Anne," says he, "I shall have a good deal of money soon, and you shall have some." And I know he soon after had a good deal of money, and he paid me five guineas. That summer we went to lodge at Kingston, and Mr. Sloper with us. My master used often to leave Mr. Sloper and my mistress at home, and go a-riding, or abroad somewhere or other. The rest of the servants wondered at it as well as I, but I knew no harm. They did not know Mr. Sloper's name; my master called him his cousin Thompson. Afterwards, when they came to town, I left the service and took that lodging. In last Spring, about March last, I lived with them again. My master took me aside, and made me promise secrecy concerning something he was about to say to me. He told me he was going to France; that there was an affair between Mr. Sloper and his wife; that he was ruined for ever if it should be publicly known; and he made me promise to live with her till he could come back, that the rest of the servants might not know anything of the matter. I promised him. They took lodgings at Kensington, and my master went to France in March or April. He was some weeks gone, and in his absence Mr. Sloper was commonly at the lodgings at Kensington. When my master came back he was at a bagnio in Goodman's Fields, and sent word to my mistress. Mr. Sloper was not then at Kensington. My mistress and I went to Goodman's Fields in a hackney coach, and he came back with us to Kensington. In our return we changed our coach two or three times by the way, that he might not be discovered. She told him she expected Mr. Sloper in a day or two. My master said he would take a lodging when Mr. Sloper came; or, if there was not time for that, he would go lie at some inn in the town. Within two or three days Mr. Sloper came and then Mr. Cibber sent and took a lodging at Blue Green ; and after supper, about nine or ten o'clock, he went there with a man carrying a lanthorn and candle, and left Mrs. Cibber and Mr. Sloper at the lodgings at Kensington. He came back to breakfast next morning, and dined and, I believe, supped ; and so he did several days, till Mr. Sloper went away, and then Mr. Cibber paid off the lodgings at Blue Green and came to the lodgings in Kensington to his wife.

Q. Was you at Burnham with Mr. Cibber and his wife and Mr. Sloper ?

ANNE HOPSON. Yes, last summer it was. They three and I looked over the house, that they might contrive in what rooms to lie, and the rest of the servants know nothing of the affair. It was a large house, seven rooms on a floor. Mr. Cibber's bedchamber and Mr. Sloper's had a door opened between them. Mrs. Cibber used to undress herself in my master's room and leave her clothes there, and put on a bedgown, and take away one of the pillows from my master's bed, and go away to Mr. Sloper's room. My master used to shut the door after her, and say " Good night, my dear," and sometimes he used to knock at their door in a morning and call them up to breakfast, and at other times he sent me to call them ; and the pillow was brought back again, for my master's bed was always made with two pillows.

Q. Did you see Mrs. Cibber the day she was rescued, and where ?

ANNE HOPSON : Yes, I saw her at her mother's, Mrs. Arne.

Q. Was Mr. Sloper there ?

ANNE HOPSON. He was there.

Q. What became of Mrs. Cibber ?

ANNE HOPSON. I do not know. She went away somewhere. I did not see her till two or three days afterwards.

Q. Did you go into the country with her afterwards ?

ANNE HOPSON. Yes, we went to Reading. Mr. Sloper met us at Slough, and there we went into the Reading coach. Mr. Soper walked out some time before us, and the coach took him up.

Q. Where was Mrs. Cibber afterwards ?

ANNE HOPSON. At Reading with Mr. Sloper, till she came to town about five weeks ago.

MRS. CARTER (the wife of a former witness) was sworn.

She gave in substance the same evidence that her husband did before, and that Mr. Sloper used to pay the money for housekeeping. That when the lodging was taken at Blue Green, and upon her asking the meaning of it she had for answer, 'twas because Mr. Cibber was a mean-spirited dog.

Q. Why would you keep such a house ?

MRS. CARTER. I thought it no business of mine, if the husband consented and was satisfied.

JANE PHILLIPS was sworn.

Q. Give the Court, etc.

JANE PHILLIPS. I lived at Burnham, and used to make the beds—Mr. Cibber and Mr. Sloper's beds. There were two pillows on Mr. Cibber's bed and only one pillow on Mr. Sloper's, but there was the mark of only one person having lain in Mr. Cibber's bed and of two in Mr. Sloper's. The bedchambers opened into each other. I never saw Mrs. Cibber undress, nor do I know who brought back the pillow every morning.

As hath been said with regard to the rest of the Counsel, so as to Mr. Murray, we shall mention but a few hints from his speech.

He observed that the Plaintiff by his Counsel, showed himself related to William of Wickham, but would have been better entitled to claim that alliance if he had observed William of Wickham's motto that " Morals make the man." The words are " Manners make the man " ; but manners are there intended to signify morals. That upon the whole of the evidence, he (the Counsel) was afraid that the Plaintiff's wife and the Defendant had gone beyond the bounds of duty ; but whatever had passed appeared not only to have been with the Plaintiff's consent, but even to have been concerted by him. That the Defendant was a young gentleman of fortune, who became acquainted with a player and his wife. That she, being mistress of the alluring arts of the stage, first engages the young gentleman's affection, and draws him in, and this with the husband's privity and assistance. For the Plaintiff conceals the Defendant's true name from the knowledge of the servants. At one place he calls him Cousin Thompson ; at another, Mr. Benefit ; a cant name, taken from a particular night in the year when they get a great deal of money. The Plaintiff tells the servants the Defendant is a romp, and a good-natured boy ; and he makes a boy of him. He takes his money, lets him maintain his family, resigns his wife to him, and then comes to a Court of Justice and to a Jury of gentlemen for reparation in damages. The Counsel further repre-sented that it would be of the utmost ill-consequence if it should come to be understood in the world that two artful people, being husband and wife, might lay a snare for the affections of an unwary young gentleman, take a sum of money from him, and when he would part with no more, then come for a second sum to a Court of Justice. That he (the Counsel) desired to be understood as by no means an advocate for the immorality of the action, " but this is not a prosecution for the public, or to punish the immorality, this is only a question whether the Defendant has injured the Plaintiff; and certainly the Plaintiff cannot be injured if he has not only consented but has even taken a price." However, if it should be thought requisite to find a verdict for the Plaintiff, we had not a denomination of coin small enough to be given him in damages.

Mr. Solicitor-General, in his reply, observed the ill-consequence of letting it pass for a law that men might sell their wives, which would be the consequence of giving a verdict for the Defendant.

His Lordship summed up the evidence, and the Jury withdrew, and in about half an hour brought in a verdict for the Plaintiff, and TEN POUNDS DAMAGES.

A SHORT ACCOUNT OF THE TRIAL FOR DETAINING THE PLAINTIFF'S WIFE

On Tuesday, the 4th September, 1739, at nine o'clock in the morning, at the sittings in the Court of King's Bench, in Middlesex, before the Right Honourable Sir William Lee, Knt., Lord Chief Justice of that Court, came on a trial by a Special Jury of gentlemen, of another Cause in which Theophilus Cibber, Gent., was Plaintiff, and William Sloper, Esq., was Defendant.

The Counsel for the Plaintiff were Mr. Solicitor-General, Mr. Marsh, Mr. Bootte, Mr. Henley, and Mr. Townshend. The Counsel for the Defendant were

Mr. Lloyd, Mr. Clarke, Mr. Murray, Mr. Dennison, and Mr. Barnardiston.

Mr. Townshend, for the Plaintiff, opened the Declaration, which was for "Trespass and Assault, in taking, leading away, and detaining the Plaintiff's wife"; and again for "Assaulting, Beating, etc.," the Plaintiff's wife, whereby he lost her Assistance, to his Damage of TEN THOUSAND POUNDS.

Mr. Solicitor-General (John Strange, Esq.) stated the case for the Plaintiff, and among other things took notice that "there had been another trial last year, for a criminal conversation, in which the Plaintiff had a verdict; that it might have been reasonably expected the Defendant would have discontinued his acquaintance there, but it has unhappily proved otherwise. She has been secreted from her husband in an obscure part of the world, Kennington Lane, never went abroad, and has been there visited by the Defendant, Mr. Sloper. That after the former verdict it could not be supposed they would act openly or unguardedly, to be as liable to a detection and manifest proof. That the Declaration, therefore, was only for detaining, etc., therefore this present trial was not likely to afford so much mirth and entertainment to the bystanders as the former; but yet that they (*viz.*, for the Plaintiff) should lay such an evidence before the Jury as should make it appear the Defendant did not keep her thus retired merely to look on. That if the woman had been left to the influence and proper expostulations of her husband (who has been ready to forgive and cherish her), she might have been reclaimed; but as the Defendant has not been deterred by the verdict of last year there appears no remedy against this conduct, except another verdict for such damages as may be a sufficient warning to him ; otherwise he may be willing to continue this commerce at the expense of submitting to small damages and costs yearly. That the Plaintiff, in wanting the assistance of his wife, has lost her salary of £200 a year, and a benefit worth £200 more."

Mr. Marsh, on the same side, spoke to the same purpose, and observed that everybody who had seen Mrs. Cibber perform must know that she was a woman of an excellent understanding, or she could never perform so well, that this good sense of hers must have caused or revived a compunction in her for the false step she had made, and have induced her to have been all duty and obedience to her husband, and to have retrieved, or made some amends for, the errors of her former behaviour, if she had not been seduced by the Defendant ; who, it seemed, had too powerful an influence over her.

Here Mrs. Brett was called to prove the marriage ; but Colonel Moreton, acquainting his Lordship that he had some call of a public nature in another place, was examined to Mr. Sloper's Declarations, but the Colonel knew not of any. The Defendant's Counsel also admitted the marriage.

Mr. SMITH, of Kennington Lane, was sworn.

MR. SMITH. Last April two women took some rooms of my wife. A gentlewoman came there to lodge two or three days afterwards. The servant's name was Allen. The gentlewoman had lately lain in, and, they said came there to drink ass's milk, and she did drink ass's milk.

Q. What was their Agreement ?

MR. SMITH. I do not know, they made the Agreement with my wife. She's here ; she can tell.

Q. When did Mrs. Cibber come to your house ?

MR. SMITH. She came two or three days after they took the lodgings.

Q. How long did they lodge at your house ?

MR. SMITH. About five months. I cannot be certain. My wife can tell.

Q. What name did she go by ?

MR. SMITH. (Here he paused.) I have forgot ; my wife can tell.

Q. Did any gentleman come to see her ?

MR. SMITH. Yes.

Q. What name did he go by ?

MR. SMITH. (Here he paused.) He went by the name of Wheeler.

Q. How often did he come ?

MR. SMITH. Once a fortnight ; sometimes oftener.

Q. At what time of the day did he usually come ?

MR. SMITH. About two or three o'clock, and sometimes stayed till ten. I don't think he ever stayed till eleven.

Q. Where did they pass their time ?

MR. SMITH. Sometimes they sat in the dining-room ; sometimes they walked in the garden ; sometimes they sat with us.

Q. Was there not a bedchamber adjoining to that dining-room ?

MR. SMITH. Yes, but they always sat with the door open. The door was generally open. Everyone that went upstairs or down could see 'em as they sat, and there was a gentleman lodged next room.

Q. What relation did you think there was between your lodger and the gentleman (whose name you have forgot) that visited her ?

MR. SMITH. We fancied them to be a new-married couple that had a mind to keep it private, but he passed for her brother.

Q. Then who was to be her husband ?

Mr. Smith. A country gentleman, somewhere in the country.

Q. Whom do you now believe to be her husband ?

Mr. Smith. When Mr. Cibber came, we believed Mr. Cibber to be her husband.

Q. (By the Defendant's Counsel.) When Mr. Cibber came, what did he do ?

Mr. Smith. He brought two or three men along with him, and took some of her things away.

Mrs. Smith sworn.

She gave in substance, the same account as her husband had done, with this further : that, upon the taking her lodgings, she (the witness) had caused enquiry to be made at the former lodgings in Devonshire Street, where they said they could assure her that the gentlewoman was a married woman. This witness also remembered that Mrs. Cibber went by the name of Archer; that the witness's daughter commonly marketed for her, and had the money from Mrs. Allen.

Q. Has Mr. Wheeler, or Mr. Sloper, been at your house since Mrs. Cibber was there ?

Mrs. Smith. He has called twice. The first time was about three or four months ago, the last time about a fortnight or three weeks since.

Q. What did he say ?

Mrs. Smith. The last time he said Mr. Cibber had brought an action against him, and asked if we could say any harm of him.

Mrs. Sukey Smith sworn.

She confirmed what her father and mother had sworn, and gave an account of the taking of the lodging, and of Mrs. Cibber's coming there with a maid (**Mrs. Allen**) and a nurse and child about two months'

SUSANNAH MARIA CIBBER IN THE CHARACTER OF CORDELIA
IN "KING LEAR"

old, named Mary. She described two gardens belonging to the house, with a summer-house and arbour
in them, which were all within the view of ten or
twelve windows of the house, from whence everything
could be seen what was done. That one Mr. Shaw, a
surgeon, came there, and fancied he knew Mrs. Cibber.
She also said she saw Mrs. Archer write in a book,
which (she believes) was the same which was produced
to her at the trial. That the child had the small-pox,
and was attended by Mr. Blisset, an apothecary. That
in a few days after Mr. Shaw had been there, Mr.
Cibber came, and the next day after Mr. Cibber had
been there, Mrs. Cibber went away.

MR. SMITH (THE SON) sworn.

He agreed with the other witnesses, with this :
" I can give no account of the times of the gentleman's coming to visit, because I generally spent all
the day in the city. Sometimes when I came home at
night I found him there, and he went away usually at
ten at night. I am sure he never stayed later than
eleven (being asked as to his opinion). At first, by
reason of his frequent coming, I believed he was a
young gentleman of fortune who had married her
unknown to his relations ; but afterwards I began to
alter my opinion, because he never lay in the house.
Gentlemen, you may remember a night of terrible
thunder and lightning last summer. He happened to
be there that night. He went away in the midst of
that weather, though we pressed him to stay, and
offered to get ready a bed for him ; but he went away,
and I lent him my greatcoat."

This witness gave an account how the clerk of the
Plaintiff's attorney came there lately to make enquiry,
personating the Defendant's attorney, which the Court
declared to be a foul piece of practice. The Plaintiff's

P

attorney said it was done without any order from him ;
he knew nothing of it.

WATSON sworn and examined, and cross-examined,
said : " I am a shoemaker. I went along with Mr.
Cibber. He went upstairs directly. He said he came
to demand his wife. She promised to go. He took
some linen and apparel. She was in bed, but we went
out of the room till she was dressed. He said he was
to dine at the Rummer Tavern at two o'clock, and
desired her to come to him there, and said she should
never want a shilling while he had it. She promised
to do so. He took her purse, in which there was
eighteenpence and a pocket piece, but he threw it
back. He had her watch ; 'twas a silver watch,"

MR. CAMPBELL (the Defendant's banker) was sworn.
The account-book was shown to him. He had never
seen the Defendant write any more than his name
several times, but had some letters from him. This
witness believed divers short entries in the account-
book to be the Defendant's handwriting, as : " *Account
at Mrs. Smith's, April* 19*th—Allen having* 20 *guineas
in hand—Left in Allen's hand* 50 *guineas—Brought
forward.*"

MR. ARNE (Mrs. Cibber's brother) being sworn,
proved the handwriting in the book.

MRS. KNIGHTLEY sworn.

" I live in Devonshire Street. Mrs. Archer (whom
I since hear to be Mrs. Cibber) came to lodge at my
house the 12th of January last, and stayed there
fourteen weeks all but a day. A gentleman came to
see her sometimes, but I never knew his name. She
never went abroad all the time. She was brought to
bed there. The christening was abroad. She had her
maid, Mrs. Allen, and a wet-nurse, and a nurse sat up
with her the whole month. She was brought to bed

on the 26th of February. They had the dining-room and bedchamber, and rooms up two pairs of stairs ; the rent was twenty-six shillings a week. She was recommended to me as the wife of a country gentleman. I hear the nurses had three guineas each at the christening, and that the christening cost ten guineas.

MRS. BISHOP sworn.

This witness had a crown from Mrs. Archer, in Devonshire Street, as servant there.

MESSRS. RICH AND MILWARD, being severally sworn, proved that Mrs. Cibber could have £200 a year, salary, and that her benefit might be worth £100.

There were other witnesses examined to show that the Plaintiff and his wife had formerly lived in harmony.

The Defendant's Counsel observed, upon the evidence that the Plaintiff did not come for his wife ; but to strip her of what he could find. Why did he not take her along with him ?

In reply to this, the Plaintiff's Counsel showed that the Plaintiff was at that time under a recognizance for the peace and behaviour to her ; and that if he should attempt to compel her to go along with him he might be in danger of forfeiting his recognizance.

After hearing his Lordship's charge the Jury went out, and in less than half an hour found a verdict for the Plaintiff, and FIVE HUNDRED POUNDS damages.

Susannah Maria, having decided to become an actress, made her debut on January 12, 1736, as Zarah in Aaron Hill's version of Voltaire's tragedy of *Zaire*. Milward played Lusignan ; Theophilus Cibber, Nerestan ; and Hannah Pritchard, Selima. Hitherto she had been known only as a singer. Handel thought very highly of her. He chose her to create Galatea in his *Acis and Galatea*, and he wrote especially for her the contralto songs in *The Messiah* and the part of Micah in *Samson*. In Grove's *Dictionary of Musicians*, it is said of her : " Passing by the songs in *The Messiah*, which call for the highest powers of declamation and pathetic narration, we have only to examine the part of Micah in *Samsom*, comprising songs requiring not only the expression of pathetic and devout feelings, but also brilliancy and fertility of execution, to judge of Mrs. Cibber's ability." Dr. Burney declared that " she captivated every ear by the sweetness and expression of her voice in singing " ; and Dr. Delany, when *The Messiah* was played at Dublin in 1741, was so allured that, with his thoughts on the Sloper incident in her career, exclaimed : " Woman, for this be all thy sins forgiven thee."

Susannah Maria was at once successful. Her experience on the operatic stage no doubt helped her, and for the part of Zarah she was trained by her father-in-law, Colley Cibber, who inculcated her in, what Victor calls, " the good old manner of singing and squeezing out the tragical notes." It was not until years later, when she came under the influence of Garrick, that she became more natural on the stage. Richard Cumberland, while still a lad, saw her as Calista in Nicholas Rowe's *The Fair Penitent*, which he had adapted from Massinger's *The Fatal Dowry*, and thus described her : " Mrs. Cibber, in a key high-pitched, but sweet withal, sang, or rather recitatived, Rowe's harmonious strains, something in the manner of the improvisatores ; it was so extremely wanting in contrast, that, though it did not wound the ear, it wearied it ; when she had once recited two or three speeches, I could anticipate the manner of each succeeding one. It was like a long old legendary ballad of innumerable stanzas, every one of which is sung to the same tune, eternally chiming on the ear without variation or relief."

The season of 1742–1743, Colley Cibber says, "opened with a master-stroke by Rich, probably intended to counterbalance the advent of Garrick at Drury Lane, by engaging Susannah Maria Cibber, who had not been seen in London since 1738. She appeared on September 22, 1742, as Desdemona, Quin being the Othello. In that season, she played Cordelia in *King Lear*, Lady Anne in *Richard III*, Belvidera (a favourite part of hers) in Otway's *Venice Preserved*, Monimia in *The Orphan*, Lætitia in *The Old Batchelor*, and Elvina in *The Spanish Friar*."

Although she was regarded as a rival "draw" to Garrick, the actor and actress were on good terms, as the following letter sent to Lichfield indicates :—

Susannah Maria Cibber to David Garrick

"*October* 30, 1743.

" SIR,

" I had the favour of yours on Monday ; and yesterday Mr. Draper called upon me, but we concluded, as you did not come to town, and it was uncertain how you might be obliged to dispose of yourself, that it was best to drop the affair I mentioned to you, so I shall think no more of it.

" I am sorry you propose going to Ireland without calling at London. I should think it would be right to see your friends here first. You don't know what events may happen in your absence ; as I have no notion the theatre can go on long in the way it now is. I should have been very glad to have had two or three hours' conversation with you before your journey ; but if I have not that pleasure, I heartily wish you your health,—I won't say a word of success, because *cela va sans dire.*

" I am,
" Your most sincere and humble servant,
" S. CIBBER."

Garrick, however. had some doubts of her powers, and was doubtful whether she was capable of playing Constance in *King John*, which was about to be revived at Drury Lane. Quin was optimistic. " Don't tell me, Mr. Garrick ! " he exclaimed, with warmth. " That woman has a heart, and can do anything where passion is required." She played the part, and with great success. Benjamin Victor admired her performance : " Mrs. Cibber surpassed all that have followed her. When, the Cardinal and others attempting to comfort her, she sank on the ground, and, looking round with a dignified wildness and horror, said,

' Here I and sorrow sit ;
Here is my throne, bid Kings come bow to it ';

nothing that ever was exhibited could exceed this picture of distress, and nothing that ever came from the mouth of mortal was ever spoken with more dignified propriety." Not less enthusiastic was Thomas Davies, who, in his *Dramatic Miscellanies*, wrote : " When going off the stage she uttered the words, ' O Lord, my boy, my Arthur, my fair son ! ' with such an emphatical scream of agony as will never be forgotten by those who heard her." There was, indeed, almost a conspiracy among the critics

to extol her. Even Tate Wilkinson admitted that
" her features, figure, and singing made her appear
the best Ophelia that ever appeared either before or
since. Vitriolic Charles Churchill expressed in *The
Rosciad* his appreciation of her as a tragic actress,
though he deplored the fact that she adventured into
comedy :

> " Form'd for the tragic scene to grace the stage,
> With rival excellence of love and rage ;
> Mistress of each soft art, with matchless skill
> To turn and wind the passions as she will ;
> To melt the heart with sympathetic woe,
> Awake the sigh, and teach the tear to flow ;
> To put on frenzy's wild, distracted glare,
> And freeze the soul with horror and despair ;
> With just desert enrolled in endless fame,
> Conscious of worth, superior Cibber came.
> When poor Alicia's madd'ning brains are rack'd,
> And strongly imag'd griefs her mind distract,
> Struck with her grief I catch the madness too,
> My brain turns round, the headless trunk I view !
> The roof cracks, shakes and falls !—new horrors rise,
> And reason buried in the ruin lies.
> Nobly disdainful of each slavish art,
> She makes her first attack upon the heart ;
> Pleas'd with the summons it receives her laws,
> And all is silence, sympathy, applause.
> But when by fond ambition drawn aside,
> Giddy with praise, and puff'd with female pride,
> She quits the tragic scene, and in pretence
> To comic merit breaks down nature's fence,
> I scarcely can believe my ears, my eyes,
> Or find out Cibber through the dark disguise."

Susannah Maria Cibber to David Garrick

" November 9, 1745.

" Sir,

" I had a thousand pretty things to say to you,
but you go to Ireland without seeing me, and to stop

my mouth from complaining, you artfully tell me I am one of the number you don't care to take leave of. And I tell you I am not to be flammed in that manner.

" You assure me also you want sadly to make love to me ; and I assure you, very seriously, I will never engage upon the same theatre again with you, without you make more love to me than you did last year. I am ashamed that the audience should see me break the least rule of decency (even upon the stage) for the wretched lovers I had last winter. I desire you always to be my lover upon the stage, and my friend off of it.

" I have given over all thoughts of playing this season ; nor is it in the power of Mr. Lacy, with all his eloquence, to enlist me in his ragged regiment. I should be very glad to command a body of regular troops, but I have no ambition to head the Drury Lane militia. What I wanted to speak to you about was, a letter sent me a fortnight ago. The purport of it was, supposing the remainder of the patent was to be sold, would you and Mr. Garrick buy it, provided you could get a promise of its being renewed for ten or twenty years ? As I was desired to keep this a strict secret, I did not care to trust it in a letter, but your going to Ireland obliges me to it. After this, it is needless to beg you not to mention it to any body ; but let me know what you think of it, because I must return an answer.

" I have no theatrical news to tell you, but that they have revived the tragedy of *Lady Jane Grey* at Drury Lane ; and that Macklin has wrote a play, which I hear is shortly to make its appearance. I accept the pleasure of your promise of writing to me when you are in Ireland ; and am, Sir,

"   Most sincerely your friend and very
                                    humble servant,
                                        " S. CIBBER.

"   I have no commands, but my best compliments to every body that is so kind to inquire after me."

Mrs. Cibber joined Garrick at Drury Lane in 1753, and remained at that theatre until her death. There she played Juliet to the actor-manager's Romeo, and was with him in every piece that admitted of their playing together. It has been said of them that they were so alike that they might have been brother and sister. Charles Dibdin says that she, like Garrick, was " the character she represented. Love, rage, resentment, pity, disdain, and all the graduations of the various passions she greatly felt and vigorously expressed." She did indeed take her profession seriously, and threw herself into the parts she played with such enthusiasm and vigour as to undermine her health. " Oh, that my nerves were made of cart-ropes," she once exclaimed plaintively. She had a will, as well as a way, with her. " She," said Garrick, " was the greatest female player belonging to my house. Whatever her object, a new part, or a new dress, she was always sure to carry her point by the acuteness of her invention and the steadiness of her perseverance." Yet to the end they remained good friends.

Susannah Maria Cibber to David Garrick

" WOODHAYS,

" *August* 20, 1765.

" MY DEAR SIR,

" You cannot imagine how vexed I am to find you expected to hear from me ; either *you* or *I* quite misunderstood one another at our taking leave, for I verily thought when you were so obliging to desire to hear from me, that I said to you I would certainly write, and you called after me and said, No, no, I will write to you ; which made me think you were uncertain how you would dispose of yourself, and would send me word, when you wrote, where to direct to you. This, I assure you, Sir, is the real reason why you have not had a letter from me ; for I most sincerely longed to know how you did, and have never failed to abuse you every post-day. The shortness of your letter has made me very little amends for my many disappointments, for I have friendship enough for you to wish to know particulars with regard to your health, which you were lazy enough to mention, yet could cruelly knock me down with hinting all our amours were at an end, and if I had any thought of playing the fool again, it should be by myself. This is so unpleasing a situation to think of, that, I believe, like yourself, I shall take care of number one, and leave them a clear stage, and all the favours they can get ; for my health is at present so indifferent, and my inducements to join them so demolished with your barbarous resolution, that I must wait for a fresh recruit of strength and spirits before I can venture upon so formidable an undertaking, as attempting to prop others, when I am in danger of tumbling down

myself. In short, I am not well enough to open with
the hounds. But when the weather is cooler, and
there is a strong scent (in case I am in running order),
I will certainly hark to Garrick.

" And now let me tell you (for I am in a very ill-
humour) that you have much disappointed us all
with your flattering promises of seeing us at Woodhays :
what is become of all that *fire* of friendship and
seeming heartiness with which you almost said you
would certainly come ? Perhaps you think such
insinuations of no consequence ; but if you could be
sensible of our impatient longings and eternal en-
quiries after you, of everybody who is in London or
has gone to London, you would be of another mind.
Besides, you have actually starved us, and prevented
our having a morsel of venison the whole summer !
for Mr. Sloper has positively declared he will not write
for a buck, unless you, and sweet Mrs. Garrick,
compensate him by your company for the infinite
fatigue he must be at in writing a note to his Royal
Highness's keeper. If you have any bowels, you will
consider all this, and generously send us word to air
our beds and stock our larder ; if you do not, I thank
my stars, I have it in my power to be even with you ;
for not a dimple (I do not mean wrinkle) in my *face*
shall you *see* till towards next Christmas. As we
have not succeeded with trying every soothing means
to induce you to make us happy, I would have you
reflect upon the consequence of provoking us, and
look upon this letter as the prelude to many things
much more terrible.

"As we are not in the least angry with good Mrs.
Garrick (who, I am sure, always does what you would
have her), we beg our best respects and compliments
to her ; as for you, though you do not deserve it,

I think before I conclude, I shall just give you a hint, that upon ordering your horses immediately, and appearing before me *here*, with all due submission, it is possible I may be prevailed upon to make it up with you ; for I feel myself very much disposed to be (though I am really ashamed to own it), most sincerely,

" Your truly affectionate friend,

" And most obedient humble servant,

" S. CIBBER."

Susannah Maria Cibber to David Garrick

" WOODHAYS,

October 8, 1765.

" DEAR SIR,

" If I had followed my inclinations, I should have immediately returned you thanks for your most agreeable and kind letter, as I was then overflowing with gratitude for the most flattering commendations I ever had in my life, but as they unfortunately had the usual effect of all undeserved praises (that is, as they made me for some time as conceited as the d——l), I thought it best to reserve my acknowledgments till I was able to express myself like a reasonable creature.

" You cannot imagine how much we are obliged to you and sweet Mrs. Garrick, for your kind intentions of looking upon us at Woodhays. To be sure, this is not the right season of the year to show the lions. But let things make what appearance they will without doors, I believe I may say without vanity, *true wit and humour* reign within ; and what is very extraordinary (though there are three of us) it will be exceedingly difficult to decide who is the most agreeable. Our common way of passing our time is

in lively jokes, smart repartees, etc. : we have it at
our fingers' ends, and are not only witty ourselves, but,
as Falstaff says, are the cause of wit in others. My
very parrot is the wonder of the time! equally
excellent in the *sock or buskin,* and when you come,
shall cut a joke, and tip you a tragedy stiffle that will
make your very foretop stand on end. As I hope to be
saved ! I have taught him to speak tragedy. We have
many other agreeable entertainments here, too *tedious*
to mention, but they are all at your service.

" And now, Sir, let me tell you, I should be exces-
sively shocked at your intention of quitting the stage,
if I did not hope that the judgment, taste and authority of that great personage you hint at, would put
it out of your power to keep such a barbarous resolution ! You may resolve to be as ill-natured as you
please, but depend upon it, there are those who will
never suffer such *talent as yours* to be long hid under
a bushel, and my comfort is, they will force you to
shine (at least sometimes), whether you like it or not.
However, I highly approve of your taking all imagin-
able care of your health, and most heartily wish you
a long and happy enjoyment of the fruits born of
your labours, and the just reward of your great merit.

" You must have more complaisance, and be disposed to believe everything I say to you, before I
shall give you any account of myself. What an
infidel you are ! But no matter—you must be convinced all is not right by my not coming to town;
but as soon as ever I find an alteration for the better
(to be depended upon), you shall certainly hear from
me. Pray let me know what notice you would wish
me to give you, and I will be sure to write in time. I
sometimes fear I shall not be able to venture on the
fatigue of the stage till towards Christmas, but I am

a queer uncertain animal, and a week or ten days often make an amazing alteration in me; in such a case you will see me much sooner.

" Do not imagine I am impertinent enough to expect you to acknowledge this or any other letter that does not relate to business. I am very sensible how much better you can employ your time, than in reading and answering my nonsense. But when you are kicking your heels at the fire, and have really nothing else to do, a hint to remember your friends is not ill-timed amongst whom no one is more warmly and sincerely so, than,

> " Dear Sir,
>> Your ever affectionate and
>>> obedient servant,
>>>> " S. Cibber.

" Mr. Sloper and my daughter's best compliments wait on Mrs. Garrick and you.

" P.S. I hope you remember that I have lost poor little swivel-eye, that was blind, and also that you promised me a dog that could see. If Biddzy has any children, I should be infinitely obliged to Mrs. Garrick and you if you would be so good to spare me one."

To the end, Mrs. Cibber remained on the stage, for love of it, since she was financially independent of it. When she was in the fifties, Dr. Barry sent her an account of Garrick's " theatrical stud and ponies that run." She replied that she was determined " to enter my favourite mare Belvidera six or seven days after I come to London. She is an old one, but I believe she will still beat the fillies as she is sound, wind and limb, has never yet flung her rider, and will take care not to come in on the wrong side of the field."

Susannah Maria Cibber, a widow since 1759, when her husband was drowned in the Irish Sea, died in her fifty-fourth year, at her house in Scotland Yard, Westminster. She was buried in the cloisters of Westminster Abbey, close by.

On hearing of her death, Garrick exclaimed : " Then tragedy is dead on one side."

GEORGE ANNE BELLAMY
1731 ?–1788

GEORGE ANNE BELLAMY

1731 ?–1788

GEORGE ANNE BELLAMY was, legitimate, in so far that while she was conceived before marriage, she was born in honourable wedlock.

The authority for her life is " An Apology for the Life of George Anne Bellamy, late of Covent Garden Theatre. Written by Herself," which appeared in six volumes in 1785. As a matter of fact, it was not " Written by Herself," though no doubt she provided the material; it was written and arranged (it is generally believed) by Alexander Bicknell, the author of several historical works. It is dedicated fulsomely —as was the fashion of the day—jointly " To His Royal Highness George Augustus, Prince of Wales " and " To his Grace the Duke of Montague." In a letter from George Anne to the Hon. Miss ——, she wrote :

" In compliance with the solicitations of yourself and many other friends, and at the same time to rescue my character from the numerous falsehoods which have been industriously propagated against me, I sit down to begin an apology for my life. Censurable I know my conduct has been, in many respects. I cannot, however, suppress the wish (for a wish naturally will arise in the mind, even of the most faulty) to exculpate myself from those censures which have no foundation in truth. A review of many years of the scenes I have gone through, and of the imprudences I have committed, cannot fail of giving me pain ; but as you have frequently expressed a desire to be informed of the minutest consequences of my life, I will endeavour to recall to memory every transaction worth recording, and lay them before you in a series of letters, continued as time and opportunity shall serve. By your means the extenuations which occur may be diffused through that circle whose good opinion I am anxious to regain, and having thus collected them for your inspection, I, at some future period, intend to lay them before the public. Happy shall I be, if the recapitulations of my errors and misfortunes, should prove a beacon to warn the young and thoughtless of my own sex from the syren shore of variety, dissipation, and illicit pleasures, of which remorse and misery, as I too sensibly feel, are the sure attendants. I will hope for your friendship, that the prolixity unavoidable in the relation of such a number of events will not prove tiresome and disgusting to you. At the same time, I must entreat that you will not examine this production of my pen with too critical an eye. The lenient hand of time has not yet been able to restore to my bosom that sweet tranquillity, which the unfortunate events of my life and the corroding reflections resulting from my misconduct, have banished from it.''

Since the autobiography will be largely drawn upon, it is best at the outset to say that though it is by no means reliable, it certainly contains information of value. Its unreliability is largely due to the many omissions occasioned by the very natural desire to preserve, so far as possible, the lady's character.

" My mother," so runs a passage in the *Apology*,

" was the daughter of an eminent farmer at Maidstone, in Kent, whose name was Seal. He was one of the people called Quakers, and from the produce of his hop-grounds, which were very extensive, arrived at length to such a degree of opulence, as to be able to purchase an estate near Tunbridge Wells, called Mount Sion. For some years, he enjoyed in comfort the fruits of his industry ; but happening one evening during the autumn to continue in his grounds, he caught a cold, which, bringing on a fever, in a few days put an end to his existence."

Seal, who was a good husband and father, did not make a will, so that, according to George Anne, the whole of his effects fell into the hands of his widow, without any provision being made for his four-year-old daughter. Mrs. Seal disposed of the property, at Maidstone, and remained at that genteel wateringplace, Tunbridge Wells. It would not appear that she was rich, for she " furnished her houses there in an elegant manner, and let them, during the season, to persons of the first distinction."

Mrs. Seal, who was still young and good-looking and had, at least, some money, attracted the attention of a person of the name of Busby. He " was a builder of some eminence, and considered by the world as a man in affluent circumstances ; and so high an opinion had my grandmother formed of him during his courtship, that she imprudently married him, without reserving to herself, or her child, by any written agreement, the least part of her fortune. She received from him, however, the most solemn assurances, that they should both be liberally provided for."

So certain was Mrs. Seal of Busby's good faith, that she declined an offer of Mrs. Godfrey, Mistress of the Jewel House, and sister to the great Duke of Marlborough, who had rented one of her houses, to adopt her little girl. Busby was a pious humbug. Instead of being well provided with the goods of the world, as he had represented, he was heavily in debt, and, not long after the marriage, the property that had been Mrs. Busby's was seized by her husband's creditors.

Mrs. Godfrey came to the rescue by offering again to befriend the little girl, and this time her proposal was gratefully accepted. Mrs. Godfrey placed young Miss Seal—her Christian name has not been handed down—at a boarding-school in Queen's Square, where her own daughter was being educated. While she was still there, she, at the age of fourteen attracted the attention of the profligate James O'Hara, second Baron Tyrawley, of whom Horace Walpole said that he once returned from a lengthy diplomatic mission abroad with " three wives and fourteen children." The inexperienced girl was fascinated by this accomplished master of seduction—where was the schoolmistress ?—and eloped with him. He housed her in his own apartments in Somerset House. " She was treated with the same respect as if she had really been Lady Tyrawley," her daughter asserts. " This honour he had frequently promised before her elopement to confer upon her, and he still continued to assure her that he would fulfil his engagements. Lured, therefore, into security by these promises, by her own affection, and by his increasing fondness, she assumed his Lordship's name, and vainly imagined herself to be as truly his wife as if the nuptial knot had been indissolubly tied."

Tyrawley may have intended to marry the girl— or he may not ; but during a visit to Ireland, he found his estates there in so desperate a condition, owing to the malpractices of his steward, that the only

way he could see out of his difficulty was to espouse
an heiress. According, he paid his court to Lady
Mary, only surviving daughter of the William Stewart,
second Viscount Mountjoy, who had a fortune of
thirty thousand pounds.

It came to the ears of Lord Mountjoy that Tyrawley
was still involved with Miss Seal, and he wrote to her,
" When my mother, or Lady Tyrawley, as she was then
called, received Lord Mountjoy's letter, she was not
quite recovered from the weakness attendant of a
lying-in; so that she was the less able to cope with
the heartrending information it conveyed; and she
resigned herself totally to the impulse of her rage,"
so runs the statement in the *Apology*. " The violence
of her passion got the better of her affection, and,
without listening to the dictates of prudence, she
enclosed Lord Mountjoy every letter she had received
from her lover. Amongst these was one which she
had received by the same post, and which, as she had
not broken it open, she sent unopened. In this letter
Lord Tyrawley had informed her of the distressed
state of his affairs, and consequently of the sad necessity there was for his marrying some lady of fortune
to extricate him from his difficulties. He added, that
he should stay no longer with his intended wife than
was necessary to receive her fortune, when he would
immediately fly on the wings of love to share with her.
That, though another had his hand, she alone possessed his heart, and was his real wife in the sight of
Heaven. That, in order to testify to the truth of
what he advanced, he had made choice of Lady Mary
Stewart, who was both ugly and foolish, in preference
to one who was both beautiful and sensible; lest a
union with a more agreeable person might be the
means of decreasing his affection for her."

The fury of Lord Mountjoy can easily be imagined. He wrote at once forbidding his daughter to see or communicate in any way with Tyrawley, but it was too late : the marriage had taken place secretly. All that the angry father could do was to withhold the promised dowry, and as that was all Tyrawley had wanted, a separation was arranged within a few months.

Miss Seal, on hearing of the marriage, of course, left Somerset House. At the suggestion of Mrs. Butler, an actress, she decided to go on the stage, and actually secured an engagement to appear at Dublin. It soon appeared, however, that she had not the qualities for success in the theatre. All this time, Tyrawley, who had in 1728 gone to Lisbon as Ambassador-Extraordinary, was writing to her assuring her of his love, begging her to join him. After a while, she decided to do so ; but on her arrival, though he welcomed her warmly, she found that he had taken unto himself another mistress.

While at Lisbon, one Bellamy, a captain in the British mercantile marine, succumbed to the charms of Miss Seal, and made her an offer of marriage. More than once, he repeated this—only to be refused. Finally, in a fit of jealousy, she accepted him. They were married, and sailed for Ireland in the ship that Bellamy commanded. " In a few months after the arrival of Captain Bellamy and his new-married lady at the place of their destination, to the inexpressible astonishment and dissatisfaction of the former, I made my appearance on this habitable globe," says the *Apology*. " My mother had so carefully concealed her pregnancy, and her connection with Lord Tyrawley, from her husband, that he had not entertained the least suspicion of her incontinence. My birth,

GEORGE ANNE BELLAMY

however, discovered the whole ; and so exasperated was the Captain at her duplicity, that he immediately left the kingdom, and never after either saw or corresponded with her."

According to George Anne Bellamy, in the *Apology*, she " was born at Fingal on St. George's Day, 1733, some months too soon for Captain Bellamy to claim any degree of consanguinity with me." St. George's Day it probably was, since she was christened George Anne—in mistake, it is said, for Georgiana. The year, however, is in dispute, for later the lady produced a birth certificate, dated 1731. Chetwood, in his *General History of the Stage*, gives the year as 1727, but does not condescend to give any reason for this. Unquestionably, he is wrong, for though Miss Seal bore a child to Tyrawley in that year, that child was a boy. The year was probably 1728.

Tyrawley, in due course, heard of the arrival of the infant, and acknowledged the paternity—at the same time washing his hands of the mother. He undertook the custody of George Anne, on condition that Miss Seal gave up all claim on her, which was agreed. The child, at the age of five, was lodged in a convent at Boulogne, where she stayed for six years. She was then brought back to London, where her father had just (about 1742) arrived from Lisbon. " My Lord's fondness for me knew no bounds," she says. " He not only thought he perceived in my features the perfect resemblance of his own, but he flattered himself that, with the aid of due cultivation, I should likewise inherit his wit, which was universally allowed to be really brilliant."

Tyrawley, who evidently—even apart from her own account—was proud of her, introduced her to

Pope, who had no use for the child, and to Lord Chesterfield, who flattered and petted her.

Tyrawley, in 1743, went as Ambassador-Extraordinary to Russia. Before doing so, he arranged that a hundred pounds a year should be paid his daughter for her maintenance, on condition that she did not see her mother. Miss Seal, who had returned to the stage, had married an officer, a son of Sir George Walter, who was nearly young enough to be her son. Not long after, Walter left her to join his regiment at Gibraltar, and never returned to her. Upon this George Anne moralises : " Such generally are the consequences of a union founded solely on passion, especially where there is so great disparity of years. By such an imprudent connection, the erring female draws on herself the contempt and ridicule of her own sex, and exposes herself to the licentious attacks of the other."

It was after this that the unhappy wife wanted her daughter to make her home with her : " Whether the distressed situation my mother found herself in, from the depredations committed on her property by her faithless husband, induced her to wish to see me, that I might be the means of affording her some relief, or whether her maternal feelings received additional vigour from her present distresses, I will not pretend to determine." George Anne cannot refrain from saying what a good, noble girl was she : " As humanity has ever been my ruling passion, I could not bear to think that my parent, although she had been unkind to me, was reduced to a state of poverty ; afflicted with illness ; and abandoned by the person who ought to have been her support and protector ; without feeling an inclination to afford her all the assistance in my power. Listening, there-

fore, only to the duteous impulse, I took with me the
small sum of money I happened to have by me,
together with my watch, which was of considerable
value, and a few other trinkets, and hastened to my
mother's house, without even taking leave of the lady
who had kindly protected me. I blush at the recollec-
tion ; as her ladyship certainly deserved a more
grateful return. But tenderness for an afflicted
parent suppressed, at that time, every other consideration."

When Tyrawley heard that the daughter had gone
to live with her mother, he promptly stopped George
Anne's allowance. Years later she met him in Quin's
room at Drury Lane. " As soon as I saw him," says
his daughter, " I threw myself at his feet, crying out
at the same time, with an emotion that is not to be
expressed, ' My dear Lord, forgive me ! ' His Lordship having raised me, he embraced me with the
utmost tenderness ; and if I could judge from his
voice, was no less affected than myself. He then
desired me to hasten home, as Quin and he intended
supping at my apartments. His Lordship informed
me, that he had received from Mr. Quin such an
account of me, as had given him the highest satisfaction ; and which corroborated what he had heard
in Ireland, from a person, who, *when alive*, loved
me as well as that gentleman did. Concluding from
this, that my dear Mrs. O'Hara had paid the last debt
of nature, I burst afresh into tears. Though gratitude
impelled to bestow this tender tribute on her loved
memory, yet I checked it as soon as possible, and
blamed myself for giving way to so improper, though
customary, a sensation. As she was one of the
best of women, I could not doubt her happiness ;
and sorrow, as that was the case, according to my

ideas, is only self-love. The living, who are left in this vale of tears, are *rather* to be wept for ; the dead, where, from a well-spent life, they have the assurance of happiness that my dear aunt had, are objects of envy, not of grief. Mr. Quin allowed his Lordship and myself an hour for private conversation before he came. And as the next day happened to be a holiday, we were not obliged to separate at an early hour. My mother was not permitted to join us ; and his Lordship gave me a severe injunction never to request that he would see either of the ladies of my family, as he was determined never to speak or to know them."

In the meantime, George Anne cast about for some way in which to earn a living. Through her mother, she made the acquaintance of Peg Woffington, and Sheridan, the actor. There was staged in the house of Mrs. Cholmondely—Peg's sister—at Teddington, a private performance of *The Distressed Mother*, in which Mrs. Walter, Mrs. Woffington played the attendants ; Garrick, Orestes ; Peg Woffington, Hermoine ; and George Anne, Andromache. " In this performance, though my first, Mr. Garrick observed that I was much more in earnest than the young lady who had been accustomed to theatrical amusements," says the young amateur. " And though I was inferior in beauty to my fair rival, and without the advantages of dress, which she enjoyed, yet the laurel was bestowed upon me. All the people of fashion in the neighbourhood honoured our barn with their preference. Among these was the late Sir William Young, who gave it as his opinion that I should make a figure in a capital line, if ever I came upon the stage."

At the age of seventeen George Anne Bellamy became a professional actress, and entered into an arrangement with Rich. She has described herself

as then being as " of a figure not inelegant, a powerful
voice, light as the gossamer, of inexhaustible spirits,
and possessed of some humour." Rich introduced
her to Quin, who was then all but all-powerful at
Covent Garden, and proposed that she should make
her debut as Monima in *The Orphan*—a part which
she had studied, or in which she had been coached.
Quin would not hear of it at first, and there was a
scene between the men. However, Quin presently
gave way, and she played the part on November 22,
1744, and scored a considerable success—much to
the delight of Rich. Quin, too, congratulated her ;
and later on gave her some good advice which she
has recorded—but did not follow : " My dear girl !
you are vastly followed, I hear. Do not let the love
of finery, or any other inducement, prevail upon you
to commit an indiscretion. Men in general are rascals.
You are young and engaging, and therefore ought to
be doubly cautious. If you want anything in my
power, which money can purchase, come to me, and
say, ' James Quin, give me such a thing,' and my
purse shall be always at your service."

Polite society took up George Anne, and she had
the happiness to acquire the approbation and patronage of two ladies of the first quality, Lady Cardigan
(afterwards Duchess of Montague) and her Grace of
Queensberry—the latter was none other than Prior's
" Kitty." She also made acquaintance with Lord
Byron, " a nobleman who had little to boast of but
a title, and an agreeable face," and had sufficient
passion for her to abduct her ; and also with George
Montgomery (afterwards Sir George Metham). " As
I would not listen to any proposal but marriage and
a coach," she says, " Mr. Montgomery honestly told
me, early in his devoirs, that he could not comply

with the first, as his only dependence was on his father, whose consent he could not hope to procure ; and as for the latter, he could not afford it. Having come this *éclaircissement*, he immediately retired into Yorkshire. The generous conduct of this gentleman (whose passion I was well convinced was sincere) in not attempting to deceive me, made an impression upon my mind greatly in his favour."

Let George Anne moralise once more : " I cannot avoid stopping a minute, to trouble you with another *soliloquy*. I think that word is full as applicable to a moral reflection when written alone, as when spoken alone ; at least I shall use it upon this occasion, as I cannot just now find another more expressive ; and beg a truce with your criticism. But to come to this same soliloquy. To what continual solicitations are females in the *theatrical line*, whose persons and abilities render them conspicuous, exposed ! They go through an ordeal almost equally hazardous to that used of old as a test of chastity. The maturest judgement and firmest resolution is required to enable them to steer aright. And is this to be expected from frail fair ones, hoodwinked by youth, inexperience, vanity, and all the softer passions ? Instead of wondering that *so many* of those who tread the stage yield to the temptations by which they are surrounded, it is rather a matter of amazement that *all* do not. Continually beseiged by persons of the highest rank, who are *practised* in the arts of seduction, and empowered by their affluence to carry the most expensive and alluring of these into execution, it is next to impossible that the fortress should be impregnable. Fortunate is it for many who pride themselves in their *untried* virtue, that their lot is cast in a less hazardous state."

In spite of George Anne's ideas of chastity and respect for that virtue, it is to be feared that it was more the theory than the practice that she followed. Her relations with Lord Byron, who abducted her, are not in doubt, though she may have been more sinned against than sinning. In her affair with Sir George Metham, however, she was as much to blame as he was, as the following passages suggest, if one reads— and in this case it is probably permissible to do so.

After George Anne's reconciliation with her father, she says, " I sat down, before I slept, to inform Mr. Metham of the happiness I enjoyed in being restored to his Lordship's favour. But much as it delighted *me*, it gave no satisfaction to *him*. He, however, affected to be pleased with the intelligence I sent him, in compliment to me, as he seemed to partake in everything that afforded me pleasure. Indeed, we carried our ideas of love to so romantic a height, that the correspondence, which by this time had commenced between us, partook more of the sentiments of Cassandra and Oroondates, than of persons on a level with the rest of mankind. There was so much sentiment and respect both in letters and behaviour, that I never gave myself time to reflect on the imprudence I was guilty of in entering into a private intimacy with a man, who had formerly declared that it was not in his power to pay his addresses to me on honourable terms. Nay, that very declaration, as it appeared to give me proof of his openness and candour, lulled me into a false security. And from that circumstance I placed so much dependence upon his honour, which I supposed equal to his sincerity, that I never harboured a fear of his entertaining the least dishonourable thought. More females owe their ruin to this false security, than to the incitements of

vanity or passion. Thrown off their guard by placing
implicit confidence in the man they love, they find
too late, in their own dishonour, that the expected
honour of their betrayers has been but an empty
bubble.

" As the regard Mr. Metham and myself entertained for each other, had now attained such a pitch,
that I considered him as my future husband, I made
no scruple to accept the presents he was continually
offering me. These passed unobserved by my mother,
who concluded that what money I had, was the consequence of my Lord's affection, which seemed daily
to increase. The eye of envy, however, would not
suffer so suspicious a circumstance to pass unnoticed ;
nor was so favourable a construction put upon my
apparent affluence, by my two theatrical companions,
Mrs. Woffington and Mrs. Ward. Being unwilling
to account for the elegance of my dress, by imputing
it, as my mother had done, to an allowable source,
they thought it could only proceed from my having
formed an unallowable connection with Mr. Metham.
Taking this for granted, they did not hesitate to
mention it as an affair that was absolutely settled."

Lord Tyrawley wanted his daughter to leave the
stage and marry. One day he said to her, " Pop, I
have got you a husband," to which she replied, " I
hope then, my Lord, you have found out my choice."
" I have given my word," he retorted, " which I will
not break for the whole world. Therefore no trifling ;
for I will be obeyed." She at once communicated
this conversation in a note to Metham, who proved
himself a man of action. " At the beginning of the
fifth act of *The Provoked Wife* " (in which she was
playing Lady Fanciful), George Anne explains, " as
I was crossing the back of the scenes, in order to go

GEORGE ANNE BELLAMY

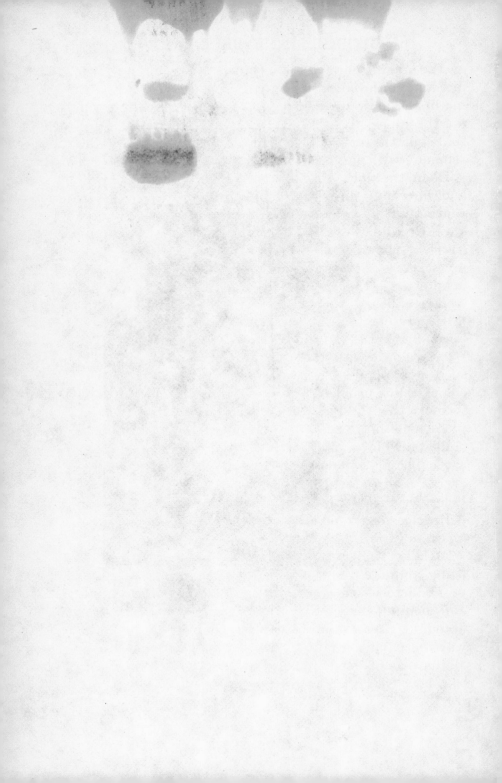

on the stage from the opposite side, Mr. Metham met
me, and conjured me to let him speak one word with
me in the hall. As the prompter never rings the bell
for the music to cease till he sees all those who are
to begin the act ready to go on, I complied for a
moment with his request. But I was no sooner got
without the door, than he caught me up in his arms,
and hurrying through the passage, placed me in a
coach that his valet had ready to receive me.

"At first I was so surprised at the unexpected *en-
lèvement*, that I could not recollect myself. And when
my scattered senses resumed their powers, I candidly
acknowledge that my love for the dear youth was so
well established, that I was neither sorry nor offended
at the step he had taken. But the mind of the enam-
oured Strephon was agitated by other sensations. He
was so apprehensive of incurring my displeasure by
such a desperate mode of proceeding, that the florid
colour which usually glowed on his cheeks now entirely
forsook them. Finding me, however, not so displeased as he expected, the apprehensions that had
chilled his blood, gave way to warmer ideas, and more
agreeable agitations. The coach soon set us down
at a ready furnished house in Leicester-street,
Leicester Fields; where I was immediately supplied
with necessary apparel by Mrs. Strudwick, the
mistress of it."

A lady who has already had an experience of
being abducted, and allows herself a second time to
be abducted—and from a theatre, crowded in front
and behind—has only herself to blame. But the
account is probably only George Anne's romantic
way of saying that she had decided to live with
Metham as his mistress. In due course, she gave birth
to a boy, George, who did not long survive.

R

Not long after George Anne returned to Covent Garden Theatre. Her *liaison* with Metham gave her a taste for expense far beyond her means, and from now until the end of her life she was in serious financial straits. When Metham paid a long visit to his father in Yorkshire, she took a house in the Vineyard, at Richmond, in Surrey, where she entertained extravagantly. She, with the Marquis de Vernueil, set up a Faro bank, and for a while made money— enough in fact, notwithstanding the expenses incidental upon entertaining the punters, to redeem the jewels, pay her debts, and have some hundreds of pounds in hand. " And had not my theatrical avocations called me from this lucrative one, it is a doubt with me, whether I should not have made my fortune."

At last George Anne asked Metham point-blank when he was going to marry her—whereupon he fled from the house ; but presently returned, armed with his brother-in-law and his attorney, and offered to settle on her an annuity of three hundred pounds a year and the sum of two thousand on their son George—such settlements to come into force when he inherited his father's estates.

" Honest " Jack Calcraft, son of the Town Clerk of Granby, succeeded Sir George Metham in the affection of George Anne Bellamy, who gives a description of him : " He was tall, rather inclined to *embonpoint*, of a florid complexion, blue eyes, auburn hair ; and taken altogether he had a manly handsome face, and a well-made person ; but from a slouch he had by some means or other contracted, or perhaps from not having learned to dance, as Coupée says, he had a certain vulgarity in his figure, that was rather disgusting. Indeed, but few men appeared to advantage, when Mr. Metham was present, as his form was eminently attracting, and his deportment truly elegant. Mr. Calcraft did not attempt to impose himself on his acquaintance, either as a man of letters or a wit. He had sense enough to know that such a deception would prove too manifest to pass without discovery." He at once expressed to the actress the disgust he felt for the manner in which Metham had behaved to her—which was a good gambit. She had received from an anonymous source ten one-hundred pound notes—she believed them to come from Lord Downe, who, she says, "had no other view than to extricate me from some difficulties, which, upon the terms Metham and myself at present were, I might not choose to ask or receive from him." Calcraft now declared that the generous donor was none other than he.

John Calcraft, generally styled "the elder," to distinguish him from his son of the same name, who also was a figure in political circles, was the son of a solicitor at Gratham who was Town Clerk, and also acted as parliamentary agent for the Duke of Richmond. The Marquis of Granby secured for John Calcraft the elder a small position in the Pay Office, where he attracted the attention of Henry Fox, at the time he was amassing a vast fortune as Paymaster-General. Calcraft, an ambitious man, saw no great prospects in the Civil Service, so he resigned and set up as an army agent. "What though he riots in the plunder of an army, and has only determined to be a patriot when he could not be a peer," Junius wrote in 1771. So early as 1757 he had acquired the estate of Rempston, Corfe Castle, and was even then credited with an income of ten thousand pounds a year. He represented Calne in the House of Commons from 1766 to 1768, but being defeated there at the election in the latter year, he sat for Rochester from then until his death in 1772, at the age of forty-six.

Calcraft stated to George Anne that, Mr. Fox, " had enjoined him, upon pain of his displeasure, and the loss of his support, not to enter into a serious engagement with a woman in public life ; and that, as he was dependent upon his patron, he could not offer her marriage. Soon, however, he hoped to be independent, and, at the moment, if she would give herself to him, he would undertake, under the forfeiture of fifty thousand pounds, to make her his wife within six or seven years. Her indignation at this proposal was, according to herself, prodigious—a few months later she was Calcraft's—to use her own phrase—" domesticated wife," and presently had a daughter, Caroline Elizabeth, by him. Lady Caroline Fox, Lady Tyrawley and Charles James Fox, stood sponsors in person : whereupon the world assumed that the father and mother were married.

The *liaison* lasted for some time and George Anne bore her lover several children, for whom Calcraft made provision in his will. She presided over his table, and, it was assumed that they were privately married. She was generally received, not only in theatrical circles, but in society.

While on the subject of George Anne's amour, let Doran, who sums her up admirably, be quoted : " What with the loves, caprices, charms, extravagances and sufferings of Mrs. Bellamy, she excited the wonder, admiration, pity and contempt of the town for thirty years. The Mr. Metham she might have married she would not ; Calcraft and Digges, whom she would have, and the last of whom she thought she had married, she could not ; for both

had wives living. To say that she was a siren who
lured men to destruction, is to say little, for she went
down to ruin with each victim ; but she rose from the
wreck more exquisitely seductive and terribly fascin-
ating than ever, to find a new prey whom she might
ensnare and betray. . . . Meanwhile, she kept a
position on the stage, in the very front rank, disputing
with the best there, and achieving it in some things ;
for this perilous charmer was unequalled in her day
for the expression of unbounded and rapturous love.
Her looks, glowing with the passion to which she gave
expression, doubled the effect ; and whether she
gazed at a lover, or rested her head on the bosom of
her lord, nothing more tender or subduing was ever
seen, save in Mrs. Cibber. She was so beautiful,
had eyes of such soft and loving blue, was so extraordinarily fair, and was altogether so irresistible a
sorceress, that Mrs. Bellamy was universally loved
as a charming creature, and admired as an excellent
actress ;. and when she played some poor lady dis-
traught through affection, the stoutest hearts under
embroidered or broad-cloth waistcoats, crumbled
away, often into inconceivable mountains of gold-
dust.''

George Anne had a temper and a tongue. One
evening when she was playing Alicia in *Jane Shore*,
the King was present but fell asleep, to George Anne's
indignation, so according to Genest, '' she drew near
to the royal box, and with a most violent exertion of
voice, which the part admitted of, cried out,' O thou
false lord !' and woke the King : thus, like Macbeth,
she murdered sleep, and revenged herself on his
Majesty.''

On another occasion George Anne joined issue
with the beautiful Lady Coventry :

"During the winter, Romeo and Juliet being bespoke by some persons of quality, Lady Coventry (late Miss Maria Gunning) with some other ladies of the first distinction, were in the stage-box. I have already mentioned my intimacy with this beautiful woman, when she was a girl, and the circumstances which occasioned it. But I had not seen her, since that time, except a few days before her marriage, when she did me the favour to call upon me, on a little pecuniary business.

"In the scene, where Juliet drinks the supposed poison, just as I was got to the most interesting part of that interesting soliloquy, I was interrupted by a loud laugh, which issued from the box where her Ladyship sat. The silent attention in which the rest of the audience was enrapt, made such a circumstance the more striking. It had so great an effect upon me, that, being wholly disconcerted, and unable to proceed, I was obliged to request leave to retire, till I could collect myself. The audience were offended at the interruption this levity had occasioned, and insisted upon the ladies quitting the box, which they accordingly did.

"A gentleman in the side boxes reproached Lady Coventry with her rudeness and ingratitude. Upon which she was pleased to say, she could not bear me since she had seen Mrs. Cibber. As this was no other than my brother, Captain O'Hara, he aloud made her Ladyship a retort, but not the retort courteous. This added to mortify her vanity, and hastened her departure. The late Lord Eglinton, one of the politest men of his time, who was of the stage-box party, came into the dressing-room to make an apology. And this he did, by assuring me, that no offence was meant to me; the laugh that Lady Coventry had broke out into being involuntary, and excited by her twirling an orange upon her finger, and some ridiculous thing that was said upon the occasion.

"The next morning my brother came, and informed me of what her Ladyship had foolishly uttered. Upon which I rung for the house-steward, and delivering him the note she had given me, when Miss Gunning, for the money she had borrowed of me a few days before her nuptials, I ordered him to go to Lord Coventry's for payment.

"Quince waited till her Ladyship came in from riding; when, presenting the note to her, she returned it, saying, ' What! is it *Mrs. Bellamy the Actress?*' To which my domestic, who daily saw me treated in a different manner, by ladies greatly her superior, answered, that it was, and that I expected the money to be paid. Upon which, turning upon him, her Ladyship said, ' If she is impertinent, I will have her hissed off the stage!' The man unaccustomed to such treatment, replied, ' That continuing on the stage was a matter of indifference to his mistress, but if she chose to perform, it was not in her Ladyship's power to prevent it.' Having said this, he left the house, as he saw there was no probability of succeeding in his errand. He, however, had not got far, before a servant followed, and informed him, that the money should be sent shortly. But from that hour I never heard anything more of, or from her Ladyship, concerning the money. Indeed I had not the least expectation of ever getting it again, when I gave it her. Nor should I have taken the note from her, had she not forced it upon me."

There was justification for her wrath anent the following incident, related by herself:

"The next day my valuable friend and patron the

eldest Mr. Fox, who still flattered me with marks of his attention, had promised to dine with me. Before his arrival, Mrs. Ray, accompanied by a man, came in a coach to the door. Though I could not imagine what could be her motive for requesting me to insure my life, as I was at that time in perfect health, yet I expected the person she should send, with impatience. Accordingly I ordered the man to be admitted, but the lady was refused, as I had given positive orders she should never be suffered to enter my doors.

"A man, who seemed to be an Italian Jew, now made his appearance. As soon as he was seated, not having any doubt of the nature of his business, I asked him what the insurance of my life, for the remaining four hundred pounds due to Mrs. Ray, would be. He appeared to be much surprised at my question. Upon which I repeated it. Then he informed me in broken English, that I was mistaken in his business. He said, the Tripoline Ambassador, to whom he was interpreter, having long admired me, and finding that I was indebted to the lady in question, he had offered to pay her the sum that was due to her, as well as my other demands, could she introduce his Excellency to me. I now found that the proposal for the insurance of my life, was only made use of as introductory to this plan.

"All the passions that ever entered into a female breast, immediately exerted their whole dominion over me. I was in an instant torn by rage, contempt and offended pride. I know not which was most predominant. They each ruled by turns. And as I had never met with so gross an insult before, the contending passions deprived me of the power of utterance. I was almost choked. As soon as I could a little recover myself, I pulled the bell; and the servant immediately answering it, I ordered him to show the fellow downstairs. The pander, fearing from my manner, and the appearance of the footman, that if he did not directly comply, he would be in danger of being shown the shortest way down, hastily rejoined his companion, and away they drove. And I soon after found, to my cost, that enraged at my not falling a prey to her machinations, Mrs. Ray went straight to her attorney, and entered up the judgment for the sum of nine hundred pounds, two of which consisted of debts that she had bought up to accumulate her own."

In her autobiography, George Anne says that on the evening of the production, in January, 1758, of Robert Dodsley's *Cleone*, she was provoked by something that the author said, " which," she continues, " made me answer that good man with a petulance which afterwards gave me uneasiness. I told him I had a reputation to lose as an actress; but as for his piece, Mr. Garrick had anticipated the damnation of it publicly the preceding evening at the Bedford Coffee-house, when he had declared that it would not pass muster as it was the very worst piece ever exhibited."

Garrick had refused *Cleone*, which he termed " a cruel, bloody, unnatural play," and on the night that it was brought out at Covent Garden, Garrick appeared for the first time as Marplot in *The Busybody* at Drury Lane, and on the following morning he wrote to congratulate Dodsley on his success, and asked him at the same time to let him know how he could support his interest without absolutely giving up his own. To this Dodsley returned a cold reply:

Robert Dodsley to David Garrick

" *December* 5, 1757.

" SIR,

" I thank you for you compliments on the success of *Cleone*, and could have wished you had thought proper to have put it in my power to have thanked you for contributing towards it ; but I think it is not now in your own to redress the injury you have done me. You know full well, that *profit* was but my second motive for bringing this piece on the stage, and you have taken effectual care to nip its *reputation* in the bud, by preventing the town, as far as lay in your power, from attending to it. As to my proposing any means in which you can now be of service to me, I hope you do not think, that after what has passed, I can possibly bring myself to ask a favour of you, In short, if your behaviour to me has been right, I see no cause you have to be concerned about it ; if wrong, why was it so ? I am certain I gave you no provocation for it. I therefore leave it on yourself to pursue what measures you may think most consistent with your own reputation ; as to mine, you have certainly in this instance done all you could to lessen it. However, I beg you will believe it is with some regret I feel I cannot at present subscribe myself with that cordiality I have always wished to be,

" Sir, your friend and servant,

" R. DODSLEY."

To this Garrick replied with heat :

" MASTER ROBERT DODSLEY,

" When I first read your peevish answer to my well-meant proposal to you, I was much disturbed at it—but when I considered that some minds cannot

bear the smallest portion of success, I most sincerely
pitied you, and when I found in the same letter, that
you were graciously pleased to dismiss me from your
acquaintance, I could not but confess so apparent
an obligation, and am with due acknowledgments,

" Master Robert Dodsley,

" Your most obliged,

" DAVID GARRICK."

The production of *Cleone* certainly made a stir.
" David and Doddy have had a new quarrel, and, I
think, cannot conveniently quarrel any more," Dr.
Johnson said to Bennet Langton. "*Cleone* was well
acted by all the characters, but Bellamy left nothing
to be desired. I went the first night, and supported
it, as well I might; for Doddy, you know, is my
patron [he published Johnson's *London* and his
Vanity of Human Wishes, and had a large share in
the Dictionary], and I would not desert him. The
play was very well received, Doddy, after the danger
was over, went every night to the stage-side, and
cried at the distress of poor Cleone."

It is to this that Charles Churchill refers :

> " Let them [the Muses] with Glover o'er Medea doze ;
> Let them with Dodsley wail Cleone's woes,
> While he, fine feeling creature, all in tears,
> Melts as they melt, and weep with weeping Peers.'

Dr. Johnson was present at the last rehearsal.
" When I came to repeat ' Thou shalt not murder,'
Dr. Johnson caught me under the arm, and that somewhat too briskly, saying at the same time, ' It is a
commandment, and must be spoken, " Thou shalt
not murder," ' Mrs. Bellamy says in the *Apology*.
" As I had not then the honour of knowing personally
that great genius, I was not a little displeased at his

enforcing his instructions with so much vehemence.
. . . The next night I heard, among the general
applause, the same voice which had instructed me in
the commandment, exclaim aloud from the pit, ' I
will write a copy of verses upon her myself.' I knew
that my success was ensured."

At last came the almost inevitable split with Calcraft. George Anne's tongue may have had something
to do with it. Her flirtations with Fox did not
help matters—not that she admits that they were
anything but respectful admiration on her part and
kindness on his. " Fox," she says, " expressed his
surprise that Mr. Calcraft did not own me publicly
as his wife. Had a thunderbolt that instant riven my
heart, it could not have received a more violent
concussion. I had only power to exclaim, ' O, Sir!'
and then I burst into a flood of tears. When I was a
little recovered, I asked him if he had not been, and
still was, a *bar* to such an union ? He assured me to
the contrary. To which he added that both Lady
Caroline and himself had always concluded that we
were really married. Upon which I related to him
all that had passed at Mr. Ganfell's. When he heard
this, he seemed to be as much confounded as I had
been. He, however, advised me not to take the least
notice of what had now passed between us, but to
leave the event to time ; as in my present situation
(I was then pregnant) a dispute, which must be the
natural result, might be attended with disagreeable
consequences. He concluded with assuring me, that
as he had been made an actor in the affair without
his knowledge, he would on some future day, take
a part in it. I returned Mr. Fox thanks for the
assurance he gave me of his friendship, and promised
to be guided by him, in a point which required so

much circumspection. As for Mr. Calcraft, the indifference I had hitherto entertained for him was now grown into perfect contempt. I had before despised him for his meanness, I now hated him for his duplicity. Notwithstanding," she adds, " such was the disposition of my mind towards Mr. Calcraft, I continued to be as anxious as ever to promote the business of his office."

As this, in her view, could best be done by making herself agreeable to Fox, there was no great hardship involved. But the determining cause of the breach was money. She made as much as eleven hundred pounds in a year : yet she was always penniless ; in fact, in debt. Calcraft came to the rescue again and again. Once, he said : " That if I would once convince him that I knew the value of money, he would give me a thousand pounds for every hundred I then required. Tired with this *pecuniary* conversation, which always was the most unpleasing to me of any, and now holding him in sovereign contempt, I replied that I left it to plodders like him, who were possessed of no other knowledge, to set a value upon such trash. Upon this, he pulled out his purse, and laying down three hundred and odd pounds, which, with the thousand and fifty before received, just made up the amount of the bills owing, he walked down to his desk ; there to bless the mammon, by which he hoped at some future period, to purchase himself a title, or at least to become through it, a leader in the House of Commons."

In her anger at being discarded, she wrote, or caused to be written for her, " A Letter to John Calcraft, Esq. from George Anne Bellamy," with the lines on the title-page :

" So comes the reck'ning when the banquet's o'er,
The dreadful reck'ning, and men smile no more."

This was to have been published in 1767, but, she says, " Mr. Calcraft, by an unwarrantable and unmanly exercise of power, obliged me to suppress it." It remained unprinted until 1784, twelve years after his death, and even then several passages were excised. As the story has been told, it is only necessary to give here one passage :

" You will please to recollect, that the first visit you paid me after the unhappy dispute between Metham and myself, I candidly told you my situation. At the same time, I added, that I was so alarmed at his passionate disposition, as to be determined never to marry him, were he willing to carry his promise into execution, though I preferred him to all mankind. Nor would I enter into any other connection whatever. Confiding in your general character, and induced by your professions of friendship, I made no scruple thus to inform you of the situation of my heart. For at that period I did not entertain the most distant idea of your harbouring a thought of love. Indeed, I could not suppose you were capable of so much presumption, as to think of rivalling a man, in every shape, so infinitely your superior.

" I then likewise informed you, that I had received ten bank bills of one hundred pounds each, in a blank cover. This gift, I said, I attributed to Lord Downe, whose friendship for Metham prevented him from declaring himself my admirer. Notwithstanding the dial spoke not, it pointed. And as he was evidently the cause of Metham's rudeness to me, it was more than probable, that his Lordship thought of extricating me by it from any little difficulties I might have been embarrassed in.

" Upon my placing this confidence in *honest Jack*, you advised me to make use of the money ; telling

me, you were sure that the person, whoever it was,
who had shown himself so generous, would never
expect a return. You then regretted that it was not
in your power to have been equally liberal. For had
you not been circumscribed by fortune, you should
have esteemed yourself happy in so favourable an
opportunity of showing yourself my *disinterested*
friend.

" I was the more inclined to believe you sincere
in this declaration, as the sentiments coincided with
mine own. For I can with great truth affirm, that
I never rendered a service with a view of receiving
a return; always considering the person who had
the power of obliging, overpaid by the internal
satisfaction which most surely results from a liberal
deed.

" I remind you of this conversation, as some years
after you brought me in debtor *for this identical
thousand pounds*. Now as you have in innumerable
instances given me room to question your veracity,
I have every reason to believe you were *not* the donor
of the sum; but took advantage of Lord Downe's
death, and the confidence I had reposed in you, to
make claim to it. For though I cannot compliment
you upon your erudition, your grandmother might
have taught you the old saw, 'Dead men tell no tales.'
His Lordship was unfortunately killed before you
claimed the debt, and to this hour I firmly believe
it was to *him*, not *you*, that I owed this mark of
munificence.

" Indeed, at the time you said I was indebted to
you for it, though I then had many reasons to despise
your meanness, I did not think you so totally void
of every principle and feeling, as to be guilty of such
an imposition, nor was it ever to be thought that a

being, who by artifice had so far deceived mankind as to procure himself the epithet of *honest*, should sacrifice a title he had been at such pains to acquire, for nothing. I therefore, as I could not contradict your claim, allowed it; and it is now too late to dispute it."

Then came upon the scene, West Digges. It has been stated by one authority that he was the son of Colonel Digges, and by another, that he was an illegitimate son of John West, Earl of De la Warr. George Anne refers to his brother, Captain Dudley Digges. He entered the army, but, owing to his extravagance, he was compelled to resign his commission. He then went on the stage, making his first appearance in Dublin in the winter of 1749, when he was twenty-nine years of age. In Dublin he made the acquaintance of George Anne Bellamy, when she was acting there. " Mr. Digges," says the lady, eleven years his junior, " who had marked me for a conquest, sighed at a distance, and covered his vanity with such awful respect, that I imagined the character I had heard of him was not a just one. He, at length, through the introduction of a female acquaintance of mine, got admittance to my house as a visitor. And as he was really the accomplished gentleman and an entertaining companion, it was impossible to resist being pleased with his company. For a while he affected to smother his passion. But in a short time after, being really ill, or pretending to be so, he wrote to me, and declared that love for me was the cause of it. Impelled by an irresistible fatality, I read his letters." Again, " Embarrassments in his private affairs, obliged him to leave Dublin. Before he went, he wrote to me, earnestly requesting to speak with me. I consented. When his attractions, his sufferings,

gratitude, pity, and a predilection in his favour, all
joined to induce me to enter into a *serious* connection
with him. This, though not binding by the laws of
the country to a person of my religious persuasion,
was notwithstanding valid to all intents and purposes.
And the connection, in consequence, made us mutually
unhappy, during the two years we lived together."
In fact, they went through a ceremony of marriage
in Scotland, in 1763 : unfortunately Digges had a
wife still living. George Anne was indeed right
when she wrote : " I was, I think, to be unhappy in
every union I formed."

Presently in 1767, when she was thirty-six, and he
fifty-three, she set up house with another, and more
distinguished actor, Henry Woodward, and they
lived together until his death ten years later. " I
have often regretted," she wrote, " that a man and
a woman cannot live in that unimpassioned friendship
with each other, which subsists between two persons
of the same sex, without being suspected by the world
of a connection of a more tender nature, and acquiring
censure thereby. I scarcely ever knew an instance,
except in the intimacy between the amiable Jemmy
Moor, whose untimely fate I have recorded, and myself, which lasted unchangeable and unreproached,
till death severed the bands of friendship which united
us." This was probably the most peaceful, and the
happiest time of her life.

The following is the will of Henry Woodward,
but George Anne never succeeded in obtaining her
legacy :

" In the name of God, Amen. I, Henry Woodward
of Chapel Street, Grosvenor Place, in the parish of
St. George, Hanover Square, in the county of Middlesex, being of sound mind, memory, and understanding,

s

do make and publish this my last will and testament, as follows :

" First, I do order and direct that my funeral expenses, and my just debts, be fully paid and satisfied ; and the expenses of proving this will.

" Item. I give to William Bromfield, Esqre., one hundred guineas, and my onyx ring ; and to my neighbour Mr. Mason Cornish, twenty guineas for a ring.

" Item. I give and bequeath to my friend, George Anne Bellamy, my gold watch, chain, and seals. And also my plate, jewels, linen and china, and the whole of the furniture of the house in Chapel Street, aforesaid.

" Item. I give and bequeath to my executors, hereinafter named ; and the survivor of them, and the executors and administrators of the survivor of them, seven hundred pounds in the three per cent, consolidated bank annuities, standing in my name in the books of the Governor and Company of the Bank of England, in trust, to receive the interest, dividends, and produce thereof, and pay the same, as it from time to time becomes due and payable, unto my brother John Woodward, tallow-chandler, at Cripplegate, London ; during his natural life, and from and immediately after his decease, in trust to sell and dispose of the said seven hundred pounds three per cent consolidated bank annuities, and to lay out and invest the monies arising from the sale thereof, in the purchase of an annuity to be secured in their own name, and at their own discretion, for and during the natural life of George Anne Bellamy. And I do hereby direct, and it is my express will, intent, and desire, that my said executors and trustees, and the survivor of them, do and shall, from time to time, receive the said annuity, as the same shall become quarterly due and payable, and then pay the same personally to the said George Anne Bellamy, and that her receipt alone shall, from time to time, be a discharge to my executors and trustees for the same. And it is my further express will, intent and direction, that the said annuity shall be for her sole use, and that the money arising therefrom shall not be liable to the payment of the debts, control, of any person she may hereafter marry. But in case of death of the said George Anne Bellamy in the lifetime of my said brother, then in trust, from and immediately after her death, to transfer the said seven hundred pounds three per cent consolidated annuities to him, his executors, administrators, and assigns.

" All the rest, residue, and remainder of my personal estate whatsoever, or wheresoever, that I shall be possessed of at the time of my decease, I do hereby give and bequeath unto my executors hereafter named, in trust, to sell and dispose of the same, with all convenient speed, next after my decease ; and with the monies arising from such sale thereof, purchase an annuity, to be secured in their own names, and at their own discretion, for and during the natural life of the said George Anne Bellamy. And I do hereby direct, that it is my express will and desire, that my said executors, and the survivors of them, do and shall from time to time become quarterly due and payable, and then pay the same personally to the said George Anne Bellamy, and whose receipt alone shall, from time to time, be a discharge to my executors and trustees for the same. And it is my further express will, intent, and direction, that the said annuity shall be for her sole use, and that the money arising therefrom shall not be liable to any debts, or to the sale or assignment of the said George Anne Bellamy, or to the payment of debts, power, or controll, or disposal of any person she may hereafter marry.

" And lastly, I do hereby nominate, constitute, and appoint the aforesaid William Bromfield, Esqr., and the said Mason Cornish, executors and trustees of this my will ; hereby revoking and making void all former wills by me at any time heretofore made, and hereby declaring this my last will and testament. In witness whereof, I the said Henry Woodward have, to this my last will and testament, set my hand and seal, this 20th day of January, in the year of our Lord 1777.

" Signed

" HENRY WOODWARD.

" Signed, sealed, published, and declared by the said Henry Woodward, as and for his last will and testament, in the presence of us

" Ann Pitt,

" E. Willett.

" No. 89, Wardour Street, Soho."

George Anne Bellamy played at Covent Garden again from 1764 to 1770, in which year, it would appear, she left the stage. A benefit was arranged for her at Drury Lane as long after as May 24, 1785, the play chosen being *Braganza ;* but she took no part in the performance, beyond bowing to the audience at the end of the evening. She had enough energy, however, to write letters inviting support, and one of these, to Dr. Johnson, has been preserved.

" 10, Duke Street,
           St. James's, London,
                      " *May* 11, 1785.

" Sir,

" The flattering remembrance of the partiality
you honoured me with some years ago, as well as
the humanity you are known to possess, has encouraged me to solicit your patronage at my Benefit.
By a long Chancery suit, and a complicated train of
unfortunate events, I am reduced to the greatest
distress, which obliges me once more, to request the
indulgence of the public. Give me leave to solicit
the honour of your company, and to assure you,
if you grant my request, the gratification I shall
feel, from being patronised by Dr. Johnson, will be
greatly superior to any advantage that may arise
from the Benefit.

" I am, with the profoundest respect, Sir,
        " Your most obedient, humble servant,
                      " G. A. Bellamy."

George Anne Bellamy died on February 16, 1788.
Her reputation as an actress was not such as to bring
her into serious rivalry with those of the first class ;
but she was generally successful in the impersonations
of tragic characters, and was not without skill in the
delineation of comedy parts. At first, unquestionably, she owed much to her beauty, and, later, to her
social position—rather than to her social reputation.
" From reigning it like a queen on and off the stage
—imperious, and lovely, and betraying everywhere—
to the figure of a poor, bailiff-persecuted, famishing
wretch, stealing down the muddy steps of old Westminster Bridge to drown herself in the Thames, who

wide are the extremes!" Doran writes. "But in
both positions we find the original Volumnia of
Thomson, the Erixine of Dr. Young, and the Cleone,
to whom Dodsley owed the success of his heartrending tragedy. To the last, she was as unfortunate
as she had been reckless. Two old lovers, one of whom
was Woodward, bequeathed legacies to her, which she
never received. Those sums seemed as life to her;
but in her days of her pride and her power, and her
wicked but transcendent beauty, she would have
scorned them as mere pin-money; and so she grew
acquainted with gaunt misery, till some friends
weary, perhaps of sustaining the burden she imposed
upon them, induced the managers to give her a farewell benefit in 1785, on which occasion Mrs. Yates
returned to the stage to play for her the Duchess in
Braganza. More than forty years before, the brilliant
little sylph, Miss Bellamy, had floated on to the same
Covent Garden stage, confident in both intellectual
and material charms. Now, the middle-aged woman,
still older through fierce impatience at her fall, through
want, misery, hopelessness, everything but remorse,
had not nerve enough to go on and utter a few words
of farewell. They were spoken for her by Miss Farren,
before the curtain, which ascended at the words,

> ' But see, oppress'd with gratitude and tears,
>   To pay her dutious tribute she appears,'

and discovered the once beautiful and happy siren, a
terrified, old-looking woman, lying, powerless to rise,
in an armchair. But the whole house—some out of
respect for the erst charmer, others out of curiosity
to behold a woman of such fame on and off the stage—
rose to greet her. George Anne, urged by Miss Catley,
bent forward, murmured a few indistinct words, and,

falling back again, the curtain descended, for the last time, between the public and the Fallen Angel of the stage."

Horace Walpole made reference to the ridiculous length of Mrs. Bellamy's *Apology* in a letter to the Countess of Upper Ossory in a letter from Strawberry Hill, dated June 20, 1785 : " Though I am no poet, yet, I don't know what I may come to, if I live. I have just written the life of a young lady in verse ; in which, perhaps, I have too much affected brevity, though, had I chosen to spin it out by a number of proper names, more falsehoods, and a tolerable quantity of anachronisms, there was matter enough to have furnished as many volumes as Miss Bellamy's *Memoirs*. Mine I have comprised in these four lines

> ' Patty was a pretty maid ;
> Patty was of men afraid ;
> Patty grew her fears to lose,
> And grew so brave, she lost her nose.' "

INDEX

A

Abington, Frances, 93, 121
Addison, Joseph, 24
Agar, Sergeant, 198
Allen, Mrs., 224
Appiesford (coachman), 212
Argyll, John Campbell, second
Duke of, 71
Arne (father of Susannah Maria),
195
Arne, Susannah Maria. *See*
Cibber
Arne, Thomas Augustine, 195,
212, 226

B

Barnardiston, Mr., 199, 221
Barry, Dr., 238
Barry, Elizabeth, 71, 87
Barry, Spranger, 77, 87, 178
Bathurst, Henry, second Earl,
50
Beard, John, 54, 70
Bellamy, Captain, 248, 249
Bellamy, George Anne, 105,
119, 120, 188, 190, 243, 279
Bellchambers, Edmund, 19, 22,
23.
Bellingham, Lady, 177
Bellingham, Sir William, Bart.,
177
Bentley, Richard, 91

Beswick, Lavinia. *See* Fenton
Betterton, Mrs., 119
Betterton, Thomas, 71
Bishop, Mrs., 227
Blanchard, Elizabeth. *See*
Oldfield
Bolton, Anne, Duchess of, 48,
49, 50
Bolton, Charles Paulet, third
Duke of, 48, 49, 50
Bolton, Lavinia, Duchess of,
See Fenton
Boothe, Mr., 220
Boswell, James, 71, 177
Bracegirdle, Anne, 19, 20, 71
Brett, Mrs., 212, 222
Bromfield, William, 274, 276
Bullock, H., 42
Burgoyne, General John, 25
Burke, Edmund, 177
Burney, Charles, 228
Burney, Frances, 177
Buononcini, Giovanni Battista,
62
Busby, Mrs., 245, 246
Butler, Mrs., 133, 248
Byron, Lord, 253, 255

C

Cadogan, Charles Sloane, first
Earl of, 29.
Cadogan, Mary, Countess of, 29